Northumberland Trig Bag

Trig points, or trigonometrical stations to give them t
sight and much-loved feature of Britain's hills. Const
part of the Ordnance Survey's Retriangulation of Great Britain, this log book is your
ideal hiking companion as you 'bag' them all in Northumberland.

This log book contains all 152 trig pillars to be found in Northumberland. Finding
them and 'bagging' them is the challenge ahead of you! Some trig pillars are at the
top of mountains, some are half-buried in heather moors or in dense woodland - so
plan your trip accordingly. *

Using the book is easy, use the map page to plan your next adventure and scan the QR code using your smartphone on the page of the trig pillar you are planning on bagging - this will open a map of the trig point.
You can zoom in and out accordingly to plan your route. Each trig has an OS grid reference which you can enter into your GPS system to follow on the day.

TOP TIP:
You can zoom in and out on the map on your phone by pressing the [+] and [-] buttons. Take screenhots in case you are out of mobile data on the hills!

Make sure when you have bagged your trig points, tick them off on the contents page and fill in the tick on your log page after you have filled in your adventure details!

Enjoy your hiking!

* Disclaimer: Some pillars are located in areas owned by the UK military and these areas have been deemed 'Danger Zones'. As this book contains all the trig pillars in Northumberland they have been included, however visiting these particular pillars is taken at your own risk and trespassing laws should always be adhered to.
Further information on military firing times & access can be obtained through the QR code or by visiting: www.gov.uk/government/publications/otterburn-firing-times

#	Name	Page	#	Name	Page
1	Barcombe	Page 9	77	Hexham Racecourse	Page 85
2	Barley Hill	Page 10	78	High Trewhitt	Page 86
3	Batey Catreen	Page 11	79	Highfield	Page 87
4	Bavington Crags	Page 12	80	Hillhead	Page 88
5	Beacon Hill	Page 13	81	Hindhope Law	Page 89
6	Belford Crag	Page 14	82	Hips Heugh	Page 90
7	Berrymoor Edge	Page 15	83	Hopealone	Page 91
8	Birk Hill	Page 16	84	Hungry Law	Page 92
9	Black Knowe	Page 17	85	Killhope Law	Page 93
10	Blackburn Common	Page 18	86	Kings Seat	Page 94
11	Blackchester	Page 19	87	Lamb Hill	Page 95
12	Blackdown	Page 20	88	Lane End	Page 96
13	Blackmoor Skirt	Page 21	89	Law Plantation	Page 97
14	Blackwool Law	Page 22	90	Limestone Bank	Page 98
15	Blakemans Law	Page 23	91	Linbrig	Page 99
16	Bloodybush Edge	Page 24	92	Long Crag	Page 100
17	Bolts Law Smalesmouth	Page 25	93	Long Crag Gunnerton	Page 101
18	Bowsden West	Page 26	94	Longknowe Hill	Page 102
19	Branshaw	Page 27	95	Manside Cross	Page 103
20	Brizlee Wood	Page 28	96	March Head	Page 104
21	Broom Hill	Page 29	97	Mattilees Hill	Page 105
22	Brownley Hill	Page 30	98	Menceles	Page 106
23	Bulbeck Common	Page 31	99	Midhopelaw Pike	Page 107
24	Burn Divot	Page 32	100	Military Road	Page 108
25	Burradon Mains	Page 33	101	Monkside	Page 109
26	Cairn End	Page 34	102	Monylaws	Page 110
27	Cairnglastenhope	Page 35	103	Moot Law	Page 111
28	Camp Hill	Page 36	104	Murton Whitehouse	Page 112
29	Carter Bar	Page 37	105	New Heaton	Page 113
30	Catton Beacon	Page 38	106	Newton Tors	Page 114
31	Chatton Park Hill	Page 39	107	Night Fold Field	Page 115
32	Cheeveley	Page 40	108	Old Fawdon Hill	Page 116
33	Chester Hill	Page 41	109	Pasture Hill Plantation	Page 117
34	Cheviot	Page 42	110	Pigdon	Page 118
35	Coatyards	Page 43	111	Pike Rigg	Page 119
36	Cold Law	Page 44	112	Ravensheugh Crags	Page 120
37	Corby Pike	Page 45	113	Reaveley Hill	Page 121
38	Cramondhill	Page 46	114	Rhodes Hill	Page 122
39	Curleheugh	Page 47	115	Ridlees Cairn	Page 123
40	Darden Pike	Page 48	116	Ripley Carrs	Page 124
41	Deadwater Moor	Page 49	117	Ross Castle	Page 125
42	Dilston	Page 50	118	Round Top	Page 126
43	Dod Law	Page 51	119	Sewingshields Crags	Page 127
44	Doddington	Page 52	120	Shaftoe Crags	Page 128
45	Dour Hill	Page 53	121	Shepherdskirk Hill	Page 129
46	Ealingham Rigg	Page 54	122	Shill Moor	Page 130
47	East Hill	Page 55	123	Shillhope Law	Page 131
48	East Lightside Farm	Page 56	124	Shoreswood	Page 132
49	Ell Hill	Page 57	125	Spy Rigg	Page 133
50	Ellis Crag	Page 58	126	Stokoe High Crags	Page 134
51	Fellhouse Fell	Page 59	127	Target Plantation	Page 135
52	Five Lane Ends	Page 60	128	The Beacon	Page 136
53	Fourlaws Hill	Page 61	129	The Dodd	Page 137
54	Freemanshill Moor	Page 62	130	The Grun	Page 138
55	Gains Law	Page 63	131	Thirl Moor	Page 139
56	Garleigh Moor	Page 64	132	Thornton House	Page 140
57	Gaterley Hill	Page 65	133	Thorny Hill	Page 141
58	Glendhu Hill	Page 66	134	Tinely Moor	Page 142
59	Green Hill	Page 67	135	Titlington Pike	Page 143
60	Greenleighton	Page 68	136	Tosson Hill	Page 144
61	Greensheen Hill	Page 69	137	Warden Hill	Page 145
62	Greenside	Page 70	138	Warlaw Pike	Page 146
63	Greys Pike	Page 71	139	Watch Crags	Page 147
64	Halidon Hill	Page 72	140	Watsons Pike	Page 148
65	Hangwell Law	Page 73	141	Wether Cairn	Page 149
66	Harbottle	Page 74	142	Wether Hill	Page 150
67	Hard Rigg	Page 75	143	White Crags	Page 151
68	Hart Law	Page 76	144	White House Hill	Page 152
69	Harwood Side	Page 77	145	Whitehill	Page 153
70	Haydon Fell	Page 78	146	Whitsunbank Hill	Page 154
71	Hebron Hill	Page 79	147	Whitton Hill	Page 155
72	Heddon Hill	Page 80	148	Wind Hill	Page 156
73	Hedgehope Hill	Page 81	149	Windy Gyle	Page 157
74	Hedley Hill	Page 82	150	Winnowshill Common	Page 158
75	Helm	Page 83	151	Winshields	Page 159
76	Hexham Common	Page 84	152	Wreighill Pike	Page 160

Northumbeland Trig Points
at a glance

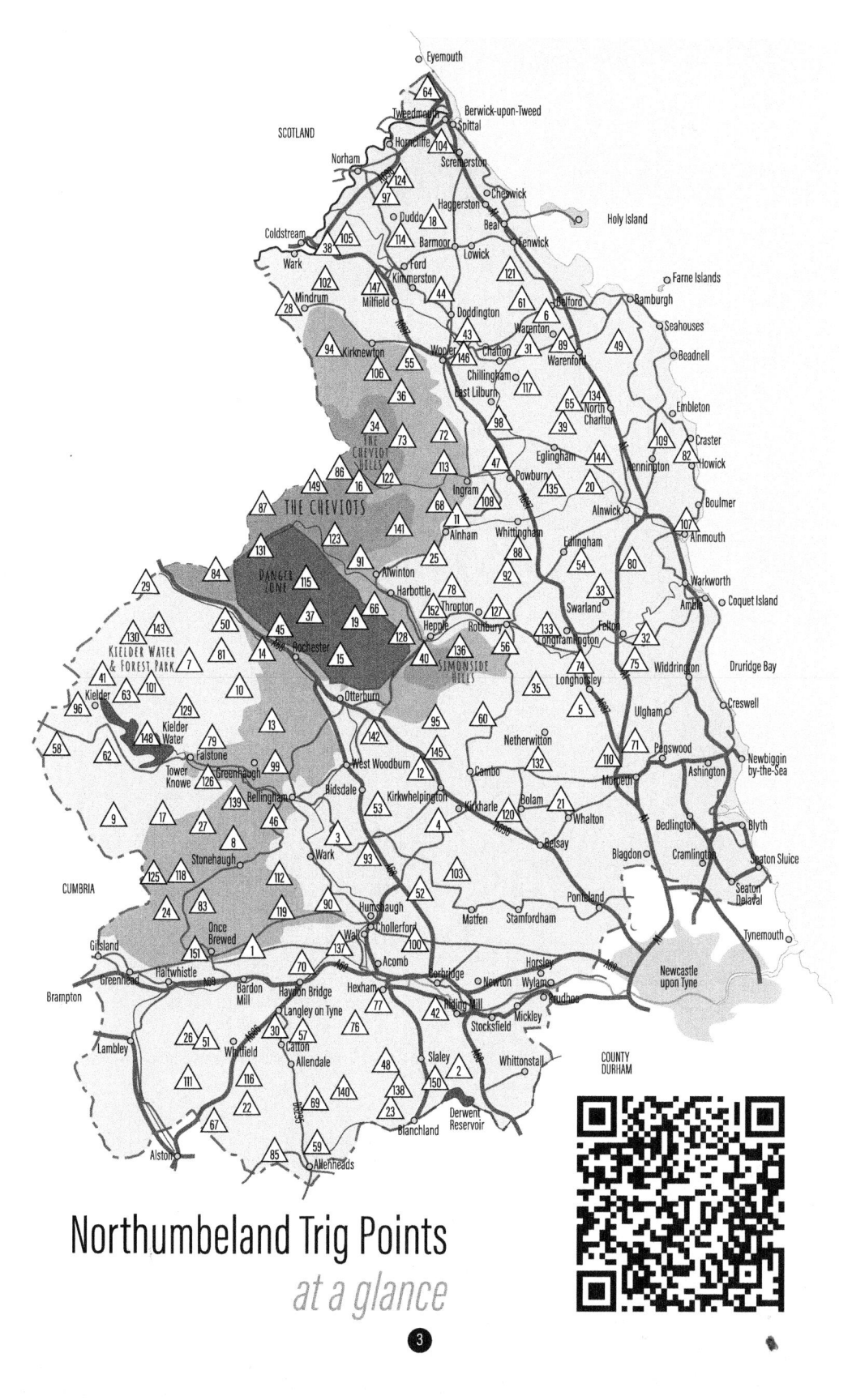

Trig Finder - In Alphabetical Order

✓	Name	Page	✓	Name	Page
○	Barcombe	Page 9	○	Curleheugh	Page 47
○	Barley Hill	Page 10	○	Darden Pike	Page 48
○	Batey Catreen	Page 11	○	Deadwater Moor	Page 49
○	Bavington Crags	Page 12	○	Dilston	Page 50
○	Beacon Hill	Page 13	○	Dod Law	Page 51
○	Belford Crag	Page 14	○	Doddington	Page 52
○	Berrymoor Edge	Page 15	○	Dour Hill	Page 53
○	Birk Hill	Page 16	○	Ealingham Rigg	Page 54
○	Black Knowe	Page 17	○	East Hill	Page 55
○	Blackburn Common	Page 18	○	East Lightside Farm	Page 56
○	Blackchester	Page 19	○	Ell Hill	Page 57
○	Blackdown	Page 20	○	Ellis Crag	Page 58
○	Blackmoor Skirt	Page 21	○	Fellhouse Fell	Page 59
○	Blackwool Law	Page 22	○	Five Lane Ends	Page 60
○	Blakemans Law	Page 23	○	Fourlaws Hill	Page 61
○	Bloodybush Edge	Page 24	○	Freemanshill Moor	Page 62
○	Bolts Law Smalesmouth	Page 25	○	Gains Law	Page 63
○	Bowsden West	Page 26	○	Garleigh Moor	Page 64
○	Branshaw	Page 27	○	Gaterley Hill	Page 65
○	Brizlee Wood	Page 28	○	Glendhu Hill	Page 66
○	Broom Hill	Page 29	○	Green Hill	Page 67
○	Brownley Hill	Page 30	○	Greenleighton	Page 68
○	Bulbeck Common	Page 31	✓	Greensheen Hill	Page 69
○	Burn Divot	Page 32	○	Greenside	Page 70
○	Burradon Mains	Page 33	○	Greys Pike	Page 71
○	Cairn End	Page 34	○	Halidon Hill	Page 72
○	Cairnglastenhope	Page 35	○	Hangwell Law	Page 73
○	Camp Hill	Page 36	○	Harbottle	Page 74
○	Carter Bar	Page 37	○	Hard Rigg	Page 75
○	Catton Beacon	Page 38	○	Hart Law	Page 76
○	Chatton Park Hill	Page 39	○	Harwood Side	Page 77
○	Cheeveley	Page 40	○	Haydon Fell	Page 78
○	Chester Hill	Page 41	○	Hebron Hill	Page 79
✓	Cheviot	Page 42	○	Heddon Hill	Page 80
○	Coatyards	Page 43	○	Hedgehope Hill	Page 81
○	Cold Law	Page 44	○	Hedley Hill	Page 82
○	Corby Pike	Page 45	○	Helm	Page 83
○	Cramondhill	Page 46	○	Hexham Common	Page 84

Trig Finder - In Alphabetical Order

✓	Name	Page
○	Hexham Racecourse	Page 85
○	High Trewhitt	Page 86
○	Highfield	Page 87
○	Hillhead	Page 88
○	Hindhope Law	Page 89
○	Hips Heugh	Page 90
○	Hopealone	Page 91
○	Hungry Law	Page 92
○	Killhope Law	Page 93
○	Kings Seat	Page 94
○	Lamb Hill	Page 95
○	Lane End	Page 96
○	Law Plantation	Page 97
○	Limestone Bank	Page 98
○	Linbrig	Page 99
○	Long Crag	Page 100
○	Long Crag Gunnerton	Page 101
○	Longknowe Hill	Page 102
○	Manside Cross	Page 103
○	March Head	Page 104
○	Mattilees Hill	Page 105
○	Menceles	Page 106
○	Midhopelaw Pike	Page 107
○	Military Road	Page 108
○	Monkside	Page 109
○	Monylaws	Page 110
○	Moot Law	Page 111
○	Murton Whitehouse	Page 112
✓	New Heaton	Page 113
○	Newton Tors	Page 114
○	Night Fold Field	Page 115
○	Old Fawdon Hill	Page 116
○	Pasture Hill Plantation	Page 117
○	Pigdon	Page 118
○	Pike Rigg	Page 119
○	Ravensheugh Crags	Page 120
○	Reaveley Hill	Page 121
○	Rhodes Hill	Page 122

✓	Name	Page
○	Ridlees Cairn	Page 123
○	Ripley Carrs	Page 124
✓	Ross Castle	Page 125
○	Round Top	Page 126
○	Sewingshields Crags	Page 127
○	Shaftoe Crags	Page 128
○	Shepherdskirk Hill	Page 129
○	Shill Moor	Page 130
○	Shillhope Law	Page 131
○	Shoreswood	Page 132
○	Spy Rigg	Page 133
○	Stokoe High Crags	Page 134
○	Target Plantation	Page 135
○	The Beacon	Page 136
○	The Dodd	Page 137
○	The Grun	Page 138
○	Thirl Moor	Page 139
○	Thornton House	Page 140
○	Thorny Hill	Page 141
○	Tinely Moor	Page 142
○	Titlington Pike	Page 143
○	Tosson Hill	Page 144
○	Warden Hill	Page 145
○	Warlaw Pike	Page 146
○	Watch Crags	Page 147
○	Watsons Pike	Page 148
○	Wether Cairn	Page 149
○	Wether Hill	Page 150
○	White Crags	Page 151
○	White House Hill	Page 152
○	Whitehill	Page 153
○	Whitsunbank Hill	Page 154
○	Whitton Hill	Page 155
○	Wind Hill	Page 156
○	Windy Gyle	Page 157
○	Winnowshill Common	Page 158
○	Winshields	Page 159
○	Wreighill Pike	Page 160

Trig Finder - In Height Ascending Order

Page	Name	Height	Page	Name	Height
115	Night Fold Field	48m	51	Dod Law	200m
90	Hips Heugh	58m	129	Shepherdskirk Hill	202m
40	Cheeveley	61m	69	Greensheen Hill	206m
57	Ell Hill	61m	73	Hangwell Law	212m
155	Whitton Hill	74m	128	Shaftoe Crags	213m
106	Menceles	78m	19	Blackchester	214m
46	Cramondhill	79m	47	Curleheugh	215m
113	New Heaton	92m	160	Wreighill Pike	219m
132	Shoreswood	92m	101	Long Crag Gunnerton	222m
117	Pasture Hill Plantation	95m	43	Coatyards	226m
26	Bowsden West	103m	16	Birk Hill	230m
83	Helm	107m	134	Stokoe High Crags	230m
14	Belford Crag	108m	156	Wind Hill	231m
105	Mattilees Hill	109m	85	Hexham Racecourse	233m
112	Murton Whitehouse	109m	143	Titlington Pike	233m
118	Pigdon	118m	33	Burradon Mains	236m
29	Broom Hill	127m	54	Ealingham Rigg	241m
79	Hebron Hill	130m	78	Haydon Fell	244m
96	Lane End	143m	56	East Lightside Farm	246m
122	Rhodes Hill	146m	110	Monylaws	246m
82	Hedley Hill	147m	153	Whitehill	247m
142	Tinely Moor	151m	12	Bavington Crags	248m
140	Thornton House	156m	11	Batey Catreen	250m
60	Five Lane Ends	161m	28	Brizlee Wood	250m
72	Halidon Hill	163m	135	Target Plantation	250m
86	High Trewhitt	165m	62	Freemanshill Moor	251m
154	Whitsunbank Hill	167m	98	Limestone Bank	251m
152	White House Hill	169m	120	Ravensheugh Crags	256m
88	Hillhead	171m	32	Burn Divot	258m
97	Law Plantation	177m	111	Moot Law	258m
52	Doddington	180m	22	Blackwool Law	266m
145	Warden Hill	180m	64	Garleigh Moor	268m
39	Chatton Park Hill	184m	108	Military Road	269m
141	Thorny Hill	185m	23	Blakemans Law	274m
50	Dilston	187m	80	Heddon Hill	278m
55	East Hill	187m	9	Barcombe	280m
41	Chester Hill	188m	68	Greenleighton	285m
13	Beacon Hill	194m	84	Hexham Common	291m
36	Camp Hill	200m	147	Watch Crags	291m

Trig Finder - In Height Ascending Order

Page	Name	Height	Page	Name	Height
136	The Beacon	301m	89	Hindhope Law	426m
150	Wether Hill	301m	31	Bulbeck Common	427m
121	Reaveley Hill	302m	124	Ripley Carrs	438m
34	Cairn End	304m	144	Tosson Hill	442m
10	Barley Hill	305m	71	Greys Pike	446m
87	Highfield	309m	148	Watsons Pike	447m
20	Blackdown	310m	44	Cold Law	453m
35	Cairnglastenhope	312m	104	March Head	454m
133	Spy Rigg	313m	15	Berrymoor Edge	459m
158	Winnowshill Common	314m	77	Harwood Side	489m
116	Old Fawdon Hill	315m	17	Black Knowe	493m
91	Hopealone	316m	58	Ellis Crag	498m
125	Ross Castle	316m	92	Hungry Law	501m
63	Gains Law	319m	131	Shillhope Law	501m
100	Long Crag	320m	95	Lamb Hill	511m
103	Manside Cross	325m	109	Monkside	513m
126	Round Top	325m	66	Glendhu Hill	514m
27	Branshaw	326m	138	The Grun	516m
107	Midhopelaw Pike	326m	119	Pike Rigg	525m
127	Sewingshields Crags	326m	130	Shill Moor	529m
59	Fellhouse Fell	337m	67	Green Hill	530m
38	Catton Beacon	338m	94	Kings Seat	532m
76	Hart Law	341m	30	Brownley Hill	533m
61	Fourlaws Hill	343m	114	Newton Tors	537m
159	Winshields	345m	151	White Crags	537m
102	Longknowe Hill	346m	75	Hard Rigg	547m
65	Gaterley Hill	352m	139	Thirl Moor	558m
137	The Dodd	354m	149	Wether Cairn	563m
74	Harbottle	361m	49	Deadwater Moor	569m
70	Greenside	362m	37	Carter Bar	579m
21	Blackmoor Skirt	364m	24	Bloodybush Edge	610m
18	Blackburn Common	366m	157	Windy Gyle	621m
45	Corby Pike	369m	93	Killhope Law	673m
48	Darden Pike	375m	81	Hedgehope Hill	716m
99	Linbrig	390m	42	Cheviot	817m
25	Bolts Law Smalesmouth	395m			
146	Warlaw Pike	402m			
123	Ridlees Cairn	412m			
53	Dour Hill	415m			

Equipment Checklist / Notes

BARCOMBE

Height (m): 280m
OS Grid Reference: NY 78191 66596
Flush Bracket Number: S6580

Date	Parking	Map Ref: 1

- Ascent Start Time
- Trig Time
- Descent Start Time
- Finish Time
- Ascent Duration
- Descent Duration
- Total Time
- Total Distance Covered
- No. Of Steps
- Companions

Weather

Enjoyment ○○○○○○○○○○
Views ○○○○○○○○○○
Difficulty ○○○○○○○○○○

Highlights

Notes

BARLEY HILL

Height (m): 305m
OS Grid Reference: NZ 02600 54849
Flush Bracket Number: S4108

Date	Parking	Map Ref: 2

Ascent Start Time	Trig Time

Descent Start Time	Finish Time

Ascent Duration	Descent Duration	Total Time

Total Distance Covered	No. Of Steps

Companions

Weather

Enjoment ○○○○○○○○○○
Views ○○○○○○○○○○
Difficulty ○○○○○○○○○○

Highlights

Notes

BATEY CATREEN

Height (m): 250m
OS Grid Reference: NY 89274 78822
Flush Bracket Number: S6636

Date	Parking ★ ★ ★ ★ ★	Map Ref: 3

Ascent Start Time | **Trig Time**

Descent Start Time | **Finish Time**

Ascent Duration | **Descent Duration** | **Total Time**

Total Distance Covered | **No. Of Steps**

Companions

Weather

Enjoyment ○○○○○○○○○○
Views ○○○○○○○○○○
Difficulty ○○○○○○○○○○

Highlights

Notes

BAVINGTON CRAGS

Height (m): 248m
OS Grid Reference: NY 98097 80827
Flush Bracket Number: S6637

Date	Parking ★★★★★	Map Ref: /4\
Ascent Start Time		Trig Time
Descent Start Time		Finish Time
Ascent Duration	Descent Duration	Total Time
Total Distance Covered		No. Of Steps
Companions		

Weather

Enjoyment ○○○○○○○○○○
Views ○○○○○○○○○○
Difficulty ○○○○○○○○○○

Highlights

Notes

BEACON HILL

Height (m): 194m
OS Grid Reference: NZ 14615 91388
Flush Bracket Number: S3694

Date	Parking ★ ★ ★ ★ ★	Map Ref: 5
Ascent Start Time		Trig Time
Descent Start Time		Finish Time
Ascent Duration	Descent Duration	Total Time
Total Distance Covered		No. Of Steps

Companions

Weather

Enjoyment ○○○○○○○○○○
Views ○○○○○○○○○○
Difficulty ○○○○○○○○○○

Highlights

Notes

BELFORD CRAG

Height (m): 108m
OS Grid Reference: NU 10310 34667
Flush Bracket Number: S3578

Date	Parking	Map Ref: 6

Ascent Start Time | **Trig Time**

Descent Start Time | **Finish Time**

Ascent Duration | **Descent Duration** | **Total Time**

Total Distance Covered | **No. Of Steps**

Companions

Weather

Enjoyment ○○○○○○○○○○
Views ○○○○○○○○○○
Difficulty ○○○○○○○○○○

Highlights

Notes

BERRYMOOR EDGE

Height (m): 459m
OS Grid Reference: NY 72405 97265
Flush Bracket Number: S8060

Date	Parking ☆ ☆ ☆ ☆ ☆	Map Ref: 7
Ascent Start Time		Trig Time
Descent Start Time		Finish Time
Ascent Duration	Descent Duration	Total Time
Total Distance Covered		No. Of Steps
Companions		

Weather

Enjoyment ○ ○ ○ ○ ○ ○ ○ ○
Views ○ ○ ○ ○ ○ ○ ○ ○
Difficulty ○ ○ ○ ○ ○ ○ ○ ○

Highlights

Notes

BIRK HILL

Height (m): 230m
OS Grid Reference: NY 78878 76932
Flush Bracket Number: S6624

Date	Parking ★★★★★	Map Ref: /8\

Ascent Start Time	Trig Time

Descent Start Time	Finish Time

Ascent Duration	Descent Duration	Total Time

Total Distance Covered	No. Of Steps

Companions

Weather

Enjoyment ○○○○○○○○○○
Views ○○○○○○○○○○
Difficulty ○○○○○○○○○○

Highlights

Notes

BLACK KNOWE

Height (m): 493m
OS Grid Reference: NY 64150 81109
Flush Bracket Number: S7430

Date	Parking ★ ★ ★ ★ ★	Map Ref: /9\

Ascent Start Time	Trig Time

Descent Start Time	Finish Time

Ascent Duration	Descent Duration	Total Time

Total Distance Covered	No. Of Steps

Companions

Weather

Enjoyment ○○○○○○○○○○
Views ○○○○○○○○○○
Difficulty ○○○○○○○○○○

Highlights

Notes

BLACKBURN COMMON

Height (m): 366m
OS Grid Reference: NY 78757 93639
Flush Bracket Number: S8067

Date	Parking	Map Ref: /10
Ascent Start Time		Trig Time
Descent Start Time		Finish Time
Ascent Duration	Descent Duration	Total Time
Total Distance Covered		No. Of Steps
Companions		

Weather

Enjoracy ○○○○○○○○○○
Views   ○○○○○○○○○○
Difficulty ○○○○○○○○○○

Highlights

Notes

BLACKCHESTER

Height (m): 214m
OS Grid Reference: NU 00380 10251
Flush Bracket Number: S3546

Date	Parking ☆ ☆ ☆ ☆ ☆	Map Ref: 11

Ascent Start Time | **Trig Time**

Descent Start Time | **Finish Time**

Ascent Duration | **Descent Duration** | **Total Time**

Total Distance Covered | **No. Of Steps**

Companions

Weather

Enjoyment ○ ○ ○ ○ ○ ○ ○ ○ ○ ○
Views ○ ○ ○ ○ ○ ○ ○ ○ ○ ○
Difficulty ○ ○ ○ ○ ○ ○ ○ ○ ○ ○

Highlights

Notes

BLACKDOWN

Height (m): 310m
OS Grid Reference: NY 96129 86632
Flush Bracket Number: S6695

Date	Parking ★ ★ ★ ★ ★	Map Ref: /12\

Ascent Start Time	Trig Time

Descent Start Time	Finish Time

Ascent Duration	Descent Duration	Total Time

Total Distance Covered	No. Of Steps

Companions

Weather

Enjoyment ○ ○ ○ ○ ○ ○ ○ ○ ○ ○
Views ○ ○ ○ ○ ○ ○ ○ ○ ○ ○
Difficulty ○ ○ ○ ○ ○ ○ ○ ○ ○ ○

Highlights

Notes

BLACKMOOR SKIRT

Height (m): 364m
OS Grid Reference: NY 82522 89983
Flush Bracket Number: S6590

Date

Parking

Map Ref: 13

Ascent Start Time

Trig Time

Descent Start Time

Finish Time

Ascent Duration

Descent Duration

Total Time

Total Distance Covered

No. Of Steps

Companions

Weather

Enjoyment ◯ ◯ ◯ ◯ ◯ ◯ ◯ ◯ ◯ ◯

Views ◯ ◯ ◯ ◯ ◯ ◯ ◯ ◯ ◯ ◯

Difficulty ◯ ◯ ◯ ◯ ◯ ◯ ◯ ◯ ◯ ◯

Highlights

Notes

BLACKWOOL LAW

Height (m): 266m
OS Grid Reference: NY 80804 98240
Flush Bracket Number: S8036

Date	Parking ☆☆☆☆☆	Map Ref: 14
Ascent Start Time		Trig Time
Descent Start Time		Finish Time
Ascent Duration	Descent Duration	Total Time
Total Distance Covered		No. Of Steps

Companions

Weather

Enjoyment ○○○○○○○○○○
Views ○○○○○○○○○○
Difficulty ○○○○○○○○○○

Highlights

Notes

BLAKEMANS LAW

Height (m): 274m
OS Grid Reference: NY 87348 95582
Flush Bracket Number: S7377

Date	Parking ☆☆☆☆☆	Map Ref: /15\

Ascent Start Time | Trig Time

Descent Start Time | Finish Time

Ascent Duration | Descent Duration | Total Time

Total Distance Covered | No. Of Steps

Companions

Weather

Enjoyment ○○○○○○○○○○
Views ○○○○○○○○○○
Difficulty ○○○○○○○○○○

Highlights

Notes

BLOODYBUSH EDGE

Height (m): 610m
OS Grid Reference: NT 90223 14343
Flush Bracket Number: S8065

Date	Parking ★★★★★	Map Ref: /16\

Ascent Start Time | **Trig Time**

Descent Start Time | **Finish Time**

Ascent Duration | **Descent Duration** | **Total Time**

Total Distance Covered | **No. Of Steps**

Companions

Weather

Enjoyment ○○○○○○○○○○
Views ○○○○○○○○○○
Difficulty ○○○○○○○○○○

Highlights

Notes

BOLTS LAW SMALESMOUTH

Height (m): 395m
OS Grid Reference: NY 69106 81826
Flush Bracket Number: S6709

Date	Parking ★★★★★	Map Ref: 17

- Ascent Start Time
- Trig Time
- Descent Start Time
- Finish Time
- Ascent Duration
- Descent Duration
- Total Time
- Total Distance Covered
- No. Of Steps
- Companions

Weather

- Enjoyment ○○○○○○○○○○
- Views ○○○○○○○○○○
- Difficulty ○○○○○○○○○○

Highlights

Notes

BOWSDEN WEST

Height (m): 103m
OS Grid Reference: NT 98518 42007
Flush Bracket Number: S7058

Date	Parking ★★★★★	Map Ref: /18\

Ascent Start Time		Trig Time	

Descent Start Time		Finish Time	

Ascent Duration	Descent Duration	Total Time

Total Distance Covered	No. Of Steps

Companions

Weather

Enjoyment ○○○○○○○○○○
Views ○○○○○○○○○○
Difficulty ○○○○○○○○○○

Highlights

Notes

BRANSHAW

Height (m): 326m
OS Grid Reference: NY 88386 99143
Flush Bracket Number: S7428

Date	Parking ⭐⭐⭐⭐⭐	Map Ref: /19\

Ascent Start Time | **Trig Time**

Descent Start Time | **Finish Time**

Ascent Duration | **Descent Duration** | **Total Time**

Total Distance Covered | **No. Of Steps**

Companions

Weather

Enjoyment ○○○○○○○○○○
Views ○○○○○○○○○○
Difficulty ○○○○○○○○○○

Highlights

Notes

BRIZLEE WOOD

Height (m): 250m
OS Grid Reference: NU 14774 13785
Flush Bracket Number: S3698

Date	Parking ★★★★★	Map Ref: /20

Ascent Start Time	Trig Time

Descent Start Time	Finish Time

Ascent Duration	Descent Duration	Total Time

Total Distance Covered	No. Of Steps

Companions

Weather

Enjoyment ○○○○○○○○○○
Views ○○○○○○○○○○
Difficulty ○○○○○○○○○○

Highlights

Notes

BROOM HILL

Height (m): 127m
OS Grid Reference: NZ 12052 82225
Flush Bracket Number: S3687

Date	Parking ★★★★★	Map Ref: /21\

Ascent Start Time | **Trig Time**

Descent Start Time | **Finish Time**

Ascent Duration | **Descent Duration** | **Total Time**

Total Distance Covered | **No. Of Steps**

Companions

Weather

Enjoyment ○○○○○○○○○○
Views ○○○○○○○○○○
Difficulty ○○○○○○○○○○

Highlights

Notes

BROWNLEY HILL

Height (m): 533m
OS Grid Reference: NY 80246 50680
Flush Bracket Number: S6660

Date	Parking	Map Ref: 22

Ascent Start Time | **Trig Time**

Descent Start Time | **Finish Time**

Ascent Duration | **Descent Duration** | **Total Time**

Total Distance Covered | **No. Of Steps**

Companions

Weather

Enjoyment ◯ ◯ ◯ ◯ ◯ ◯ ◯ ◯ ◯ ◯
Views   ◯ ◯ ◯ ◯ ◯ ◯ ◯ ◯ ◯ ◯
Difficulty ◯ ◯ ◯ ◯ ◯ ◯ ◯ ◯ ◯ ◯

Highlights

Notes

BULBECK COMMON

Height (m): 427m
OS Grid Reference: NY 92653 50496
Flush Bracket Number: S6696

Date	Parking ★ ★ ★ ★ ★	Map Ref: /23\

Ascent Start Time | **Trig Time**

Descent Start Time | **Finish Time**

Ascent Duration | **Descent Duration** | **Total Time**

Total Distance Covered | **No. Of Steps**

Companions

Weather

Enjoyment ○ ○ ○ ○ ○ ○ ○ ○ ○ ○
Views ○ ○ ○ ○ ○ ○ ○ ○ ○ ○
Difficulty ○ ○ ○ ○ ○ ○ ○ ○ ○ ○

Highlights

Notes

BURN DIVOT

Height (m): 258m
OS Grid Reference: NY 69395 70843
Flush Bracket Number: S6485

Date	Parking ★ ★ ★ ★ ★	Map Ref: 24
Ascent Start Time		Trig Time
Descent Start Time		Finish Time
Ascent Duration	Descent Duration	Total Time
Total Distance Covered		No. Of Steps
Companions		

Weather

Enjoyment ○ ○ ○ ○ ○ ○ ○ ○ ○ ○
Views ○ ○ ○ ○ ○ ○ ○ ○ ○ ○
Difficulty ○ ○ ○ ○ ○ ○ ○ ○ ○ ○

Highlights

Notes

BURRADON MAINS

Height (m): 236m
OS Grid Reference: NT 97116 07045
Flush Bracket Number: S7920

| Date | Parking ★★★★★ | Map Ref: /25\ |

Ascent Start Time		Trig Time	
Descent Start Time		Finish Time	
Ascent Duration	Descent Duration		Total Time
Total Distance Covered			No. Of Steps

Companions

Weather

Enjoyment ○○○○○○○○○○
Views ○○○○○○○○○○
Difficulty ○○○○○○○○○○

Highlights

Notes

CAIRN END

Height (m): 304m
OS Grid Reference: NY 71932 60671
Flush Bracket Number: S6441

Date	Parking ★★★★★	Map Ref: /26\
Ascent Start Time		Trig Time
Descent Start Time		Finish Time
Ascent Duration	Descent Duration	Total Time
Total Distance Covered		No. Of Steps
Companions		

Weather

Enjoyment ○○○○○○○○○○
Views ○○○○○○○○○○
Difficulty ○○○○○○○○○○

Highlights

Notes

CAIRNGLASTENHOPE

Height (m): 312m
OS Grid Reference: NY 75246 80274
Flush Bracket Number: S6585

Date	Parking ★ ★ ★ ★ ★	Map Ref: /27\

Ascent Start Time | **Trig Time**

Descent Start Time | **Finish Time**

Ascent Duration | **Descent Duration** | **Total Time**

Total Distance Covered | **No. Of Steps**

Companions

Weather

Enjoyment ○○○○○○○○○○
Views ○○○○○○○○○○
Difficulty ○○○○○○○○○○

Highlights

Notes

CAMP HILL

Height (m): 200m
OS Grid Reference: NT 82452 32461
Flush Bracket Number: S7386

Date	Parking ★★★★★	Map Ref: /28\

Ascent Start Time	Trig Time

Descent Start Time	Finish Time

Ascent Duration	Descent Duration	Total Time

Total Distance Covered	No. Of Steps

Companions

Weather

Enjoyment ○○○○○○○○○○
Views ○○○○○○○○○○
Difficulty ○○○○○○○○○○

Highlights

Notes

CARTER BAR

Height (m): 579m
OS Grid Reference: NT 68230 05243
Flush Bracket Number: S7500

Date

Parking ★ ★ ★ ★ ★

Map Ref: 29

Ascent Start Time

Trig Time

Descent Start Time

Finish Time

Ascent Duration

Descent Duration

Total Time

Total Distance Covered

No. Of Steps

Companions

Weather

Enjoyment ○○○○○○○○○○
Views ○○○○○○○○○○
Difficulty ○○○○○○○○○○

Highlights

Notes

CATTON BEACON

Height (m): 338m
OS Grid Reference: NY 82211 59266
Flush Bracket Number: S6655

Date	Parking	Map Ref: /30\
Ascent Start Time		Trig Time
Descent Start Time		Finish Time
Ascent Duration	Descent Duration	Total Time
Total Distance Covered		No. Of Steps
Companions		
Weather		

Enjoyment ○○○○○○○○○○
Views ○○○○○○○○○○
Difficulty ○○○○○○○○○○

Highlights

Notes

CHATTON PARK HILL

Height (m): 184m
OS Grid Reference: NU 07321 29290
Flush Bracket Number: S3575

Date	Parking ★★★★★	Map Ref: /31\

Ascent Start Time	Trig Time

Descent Start Time	Finish Time

Ascent Duration	Descent Duration	Total Time

Total Distance Covered	No. Of Steps

Companions

Weather

Enjoyment ○○○○○○○○○○
Views ○○○○○○○○○○
Difficulty ○○○○○○○○○○

Highlights

Notes

CHEEVELEY

Height (m): 61m
OS Grid Reference: NZ 21306 99580
Flush Bracket Number: S3683

Date	Parking ☆☆☆☆☆	Map Ref: /32\

Ascent Start Time | Trig Time

Descent Start Time | Finish Time

Ascent Duration | Descent Duration | Total Time

Total Distance Covered | No. Of Steps

Companions

Weather

Enjoyment ○○○○○○○○○○
Views ○○○○○○○○○○
Difficulty ○○○○○○○○○○

Highlights

Notes

CHESTER HILL

Height (m): 188m
OS Grid Reference: NU 16141 04384
Flush Bracket Number: S9540

| Date | Parking ★ ★ ★ ★ ★ | Map Ref: /33\ |

Ascent Start Time | Trig Time

Descent Start Time | Finish Time

Ascent Duration | Descent Duration | Total Time

Total Distance Covered | No. Of Steps

Companions

Weather

Enjoyment ○○○○○○○○○○
Views ○○○○○○○○○○
Difficulty ○○○○○○○○○○

Highlights

Notes

CHEVIOT

Height (m): 817m
OS Grid Reference: NT 90905 20525
Flush Bracket Number: S1560

Date: 16th June 2022
Parking: ★★★★ ✓
Map Ref: 34

Ascent Start Time: 11am
Trig Time: 2pm
Descent Start Time: 2.10pm
Finish Time: 3.10pm

Ascent Duration:
Descent Duration:
Total Time:

Total Distance Covered: 9.2 miles
No. Of Steps: 24,500

Companions: Lucy

Weather: Sunny & Cloudy

Enjoyment: ○○○○○○○○○✗
Views: ○○○○○○○○✗○
Difficulty: ○○○○○○✗○○○

Highlights:

Notes:

COATYARDS

Height (m): 226m
OS Grid Reference: NZ 08720 94452
Flush Bracket Number: S3623

Date

Parking ★ ★ ★ ★ ★

Map Ref: /35\

Ascent Start Time

Trig Time

Descent Start Time

Finish Time

Ascent Duration

Descent Duration

Total Time

Total Distance Covered

No. Of Steps

Companions

Weather

Enjoyment ○ ○ ○ ○ ○ ○ ○ ○ ○ ○
Views ○ ○ ○ ○ ○ ○ ○ ○ ○ ○
Difficulty ○ ○ ○ ○ ○ ○ ○ ○ ○ ○

Highlights

Notes

COLD LAW

Height (m): 453m
OS Grid Reference: NT 95377 23879
Flush Bracket Number: S8033

Date	Parking ☆☆☆☆☆	Map Ref: 36
Ascent Start Time		Trig Time
Descent Start Time		Finish Time
Ascent Duration	Descent Duration	Total Time
Total Distance Covered		No. Of Steps

Companions

Weather

Enjoyment ○○○○○○○○○○
Views ○○○○○○○○○○
Difficulty ○○○○○○○○○○

Highlights

Notes

CORBY PIKE

Height (m): 369m
OS Grid Reference: NT 84367 01432
Flush Bracket Number: S7922

Date	Parking ★★★★★	Map Ref: /37\
Ascent Start Time		Trig Time
Descent Start Time		Finish Time
Ascent Duration	Descent Duration	Total Time
Total Distance Covered		No. Of Steps
Companions		

Weather

Enjoyment ○○○○○○○○○○
Views ○○○○○○○○○○
Difficulty ○○○○○○○○○○

Highlights

Notes

CRAMONDHILL

Height (m): 79m
OS Grid Reference: NT 87062 40087
Flush Bracket Number: S7388

Date	Parking ★ ★ ★ ★ ★	Map Ref: /38\
Ascent Start Time		Trig Time
Descent Start Time		Finish Time
Ascent Duration	Descent Duration	Total Time
Total Distance Covered		No. Of Steps
Companions		

Weather

Enjoment ◯ ◯ ◯ ◯ ◯ ◯ ◯ ◯
Views ◯ ◯ ◯ ◯ ◯ ◯ ◯ ◯
Difficulty ◯ ◯ ◯ ◯ ◯ ◯ ◯ ◯

Highlights

Notes

CURLEHEUGH

Height (m): 215m
OS Grid Reference: NU 10917 21046
Flush Bracket Number: S3565

| Date | Parking ★ ★ ★ ★ ★ | Map Ref: /39\ |

Ascent Start Time | **Trig Time**

Descent Start Time | **Finish Time**

Ascent Duration | **Descent Duration** | **Total Time**

Total Distance Covered | **No. Of Steps**

Companions

Weather

Enjoyment ○○○○○○○○○○
Views ○○○○○○○○○○
Difficulty ○○○○○○○○○○

Highlights

Notes

DARDEN PIKE

Height (m): 375m
OS Grid Reference: NY 96812 95555
Flush Bracket Number: S6635

| Date | Parking ★ ★ ★ ★ ★ | Map Ref: /40 |

Ascent Start Time | Trig Time

Descent Start Time | Finish Time

Ascent Duration | Descent Duration | Total Time

Total Distance Covered | No. Of Steps

Companions

Weather

Enjoyment ○ ○ ○ ○ ○ ○ ○ ○ ○ ○
Views ○ ○ ○ ○ ○ ○ ○ ○ ○ ○
Difficulty ○ ○ ○ ○ ○ ○ ○ ○ ○ ○

Highlights

Notes

DEADWATER MOOR

Height (m): 569m
OS Grid Reference: NY 62570 97174
Flush Bracket Number: S7917

Date	Parking ★★★★★	Map Ref: 41
Ascent Start Time	Trig Time	
Descent Start Time	Finish Time	
Ascent Duration	Descent Duration	Total Time
Total Distance Covered		No. Of Steps

Companions

Weather

Enjoyment ○○○○○○○○○○
Views ○○○○○○○○○○
Difficulty ○○○○○○○○○○

Highlights

Notes

DILSTON

Height (m): 187m
OS Grid Reference: NY 98160 62138
Flush Bracket Number: S6500

Date	Parking	Map Ref: 42
Ascent Start Time		Trig Time
Descent Start Time		Finish Time
Ascent Duration	Descent Duration	Total Time
Total Distance Covered		No. Of Steps
Companions		

Weather

Enjoyment ○○○○○○○○○○
Views ○○○○○○○○○○
Difficulty ○○○○○○○○○○

Highlights

Notes

DOD LAW

Height (m): 200m
OS Grid Reference: NU 00686 31664
Flush Bracket Number: S3695

| Date | Parking ★ ★ ★ ★ ★ | Map Ref: 43 |

Ascent Start Time | **Trig Time**

Descent Start Time | **Finish Time**

Ascent Duration | **Descent Duration** | **Total Time**

Total Distance Covered | **No. Of Steps**

Companions

Weather

- Enjoyment ○○○○○○○○○○
- Views ○○○○○○○○○○
- Difficulty ○○○○○○○○○○

Highlights

Notes

DODDINGTON

Height (m): 180m
OS Grid Reference: NT 98906 35872
Flush Bracket Number: S7472

Date	Parking ★★★★★	Map Ref: /44\

Ascent Start Time	Trig Time

Descent Start Time	Finish Time

Ascent Duration	Descent Duration	Total Time

Total Distance Covered	No. Of Steps

Companions

Weather

Enjoyment ○○○○○○○○○○
Views ○○○○○○○○○○
Difficulty ○○○○○○○○○○

Highlights

Notes

DOUR HILL

Height (m): 415m
OS Grid Reference: NT 79562 02298
Flush Bracket Number: S7697

Date	Parking	Map Ref: /45

Ascent Start Time | **Trig Time**

Descent Start Time | **Finish Time**

Ascent Duration | **Descent Duration** | **Total Time**

Total Distance Covered | **No. Of Steps**

Companions

Weather

Enjoyment
Views
Difficulty

Highlights

Notes

EALINGHAM RIGG

Height (m): 241m
OS Grid Reference: NY 82924 81494
Flush Bracket Number: S6638

Date	Parking ★★★★★	Map Ref: /46\

Ascent Start Time	Trig Time

Descent Start Time	Finish Time

Ascent Duration	Descent Duration	Total Time

Total Distance Covered	No. Of Steps

Companions

Weather

Enjoyment ○○○○○○○○○○
Views ○○○○○○○○○○
Difficulty ○○○○○○○○○○

Highlights

Notes

EAST HILL

Height (m): 187m
OS Grid Reference: NU 04630 18094
Flush Bracket Number: S3557

| Date | Parking ★ ★ ★ ★ ★ | Map Ref: 47 |

Ascent Start Time | Trig Time

Descent Start Time | Finish Time

Ascent Duration | Descent Duration | Total Time

Total Distance Covered | No. Of Steps

Companions

Weather

Enjoyment ○ ○ ○ ○ ○ ○ ○ ○ ○ ○
Views ○ ○ ○ ○ ○ ○ ○ ○ ○ ○
Difficulty ○ ○ ○ ○ ○ ○ ○ ○ ○ ○

Highlights

Notes

EAST LIGHTSIDE FARM

Height (m): 246m
OS Grid Reference: NY 91301 56871
Flush Bracket Number: S6487

| Date | Parking ☆☆☆☆☆ | Map Ref: /48\ |

Ascent Start Time | **Trig Time**

Descent Start Time | **Finish Time**

Ascent Duration | **Descent Duration** | **Total Time**

Total Distance Covered | **No. Of Steps**

Companions

Weather

Enjoyment ○○○○○○○○○○
Views ○○○○○○○○○○
Difficulty ○○○○○○○○○○

Highlights

Notes

ELL HILL

Height (m): 61m
OS Grid Reference: NU 16807 30270
Flush Bracket Number: S3568

Date	Parking	Map Ref: /49/

Ascent Start Time | **Trig Time**

Descent Start Time | **Finish Time**

Ascent Duration | **Descent Duration** | **Total Time**

Total Distance Covered | **No. Of Steps**

Companions

Weather

Enjoyment ○○○○○○○○○○
Views ○○○○○○○○○○
Difficulty ○○○○○○○○○○

Highlights

Notes

ELLIS CRAG

Height (m): 498m
OS Grid Reference: NT 74733 01206
Flush Bracket Number: S7911

Map Ref: /50\

Date	Parking ★★★★★
Ascent Start Time	Trig Time
Descent Start Time	Finish Time
Ascent Duration	Descent Duration	Total Time
Total Distance Covered	No. Of Steps
Companions	

Weather

Enjoment ○○○○○○○○○○
Views ○○○○○○○○○○
Difficulty ○○○○○○○○○○

Highlights

Notes

FELLHOUSE FELL

Height (m): 337m
OS Grid Reference: NY 76462 59445
Flush Bracket Number: S6486

| Date | Parking ★ ★ ★ ★ ★ | Map Ref: /51\ |

Ascent Start Time | **Trig Time**

Descent Start Time | **Finish Time**

Ascent Duration | **Descent Duration** | **Total Time**

Total Distance Covered | **No. Of Steps**

Companions

Weather

Enjoyment ○ ○ ○ ○ ○ ○ ○ ○ ○ ○
Views ○ ○ ○ ○ ○ ○ ○ ○ ○ ○
Difficulty ○ ○ ○ ○ ○ ○ ○ ○ ○ ○

Highlights

Notes

FIVE LANE ENDS

Height (m): 161m
OS Grid Reference: NY 95631 74345
Flush Bracket Number: S6654

Date	Parking ★★★★★	Map Ref: /52
Ascent Start Time		Trig Time
Descent Start Time		Finish Time
Ascent Duration	Descent Duration	Total Time
Total Distance Covered		No. Of Steps
Companions		

Weather

Enjoyment ○○○○○○○○○○
Views ○○○○○○○○○○
Difficulty ○○○○○○○○○○

Highlights

Notes

FOURLAWS HILL

Height (m): 343m
OS Grid Reference: NY 91290 83667
Flush Bracket Number: S6629

Date	Parking ★★★★★	Map Ref: /53\

Ascent Start Time | **Trig Time**

Descent Start Time | **Finish Time**

Ascent Duration | **Descent Duration** | **Total Time**

Total Distance Covered | **No. Of Steps**

Companions

Weather

Enjoyment ○○○○○○○○○○
Views ○○○○○○○○○○
Difficulty ○○○○○○○○○○

Highlights

Notes

FREEMANSHILL MOOR

Height (m): 251m
OS Grid Reference: NU 14130 09371
Flush Bracket Number: S3571

Date	Parking ☆☆☆☆☆	Map Ref: /54\
Ascent Start Time		Trig Time
Descent Start Time		Finish Time
Ascent Duration	Descent Duration	Total Time
Total Distance Covered		No. Of Steps

Companions

Weather

Enjoyment ○○○○○○○○○○
Views   ○○○○○○○○○○
Difficulty ○○○○○○○○○○

Highlights

Notes

GAINS LAW

Height (m): 319m
OS Grid Reference: NT 95588 28164
Flush Bracket Number: S7469

| Date | Parking ☆☆☆☆☆ | Map Ref: /55\ |

Ascent Start Time | **Trig Time**

Descent Start Time | **Finish Time**

Ascent Duration | **Descent Duration** | **Total Time**

Total Distance Covered | **No. Of Steps**

Companions

Weather

Enjoyment ○○○○○○○○○○
Views ○○○○○○○○○○
Difficulty ○○○○○○○○○○

Highlights

Notes

GARLEIGH MOOR

Height (m): 268m
OS Grid Reference: NZ 06093 99148
Flush Bracket Number: S3696

Date	Parking	Map Ref: /56

Ascent Start Time	Trig Time

Descent Start Time	Finish Time

Ascent Duration	Descent Duration	Total Time

Total Distance Covered	No. Of Steps

Companions

Weather

Enjoyment ○ ○ ○ ○ ○ ○ ○ ○ ○ ○
Views   ○ ○ ○ ○ ○ ○ ○ ○ ○ ○
Difficulty ○ ○ ○ ○ ○ ○ ○ ○ ○ ○

Highlights

Notes

GATERLEY HILL

Height (m): 352m
OS Grid Reference: NY 84882 58312
Flush Bracket Number: S6228

Date

Parking ★★★★★

Map Ref: 57

Ascent Start Time

Trig Time

Descent Start Time

Finish Time

Ascent Duration

Descent Duration

Total Time

Total Distance Covered

No. Of Steps

Companions

Weather

Enjoyment ○○○○○○○○○○
Views ○○○○○○○○○○
Difficulty ○○○○○○○○○○

Highlights

Notes

GLENDHU HILL

Height (m): 514m
OS Grid Reference: NY 56812 86376
Flush Bracket Number: S7998

| Date | Parking | Map Ref: 58 |

Ascent Start Time | Trig Time

Descent Start Time | Finish Time

Ascent Duration | Descent Duration | Total Time

Total Distance Covered | No. Of Steps

Companions

Weather

Enjoyment ◯ ◯ ◯ ◯ ◯ ◯ ◯ ◯ ◯ ◯
Views ◯ ◯ ◯ ◯ ◯ ◯ ◯ ◯ ◯ ◯
Difficulty ◯ ◯ ◯ ◯ ◯ ◯ ◯ ◯ ◯ ◯

Highlights

Notes

GREEN HILL

Height (m): 530m
OS Grid Reference: NY 86492 47594
Flush Bracket Number: S6658

| Date | Parking ★ ★ ★ ★ ★ | Map Ref: /59\ |

Ascent Start Time	Trig Time
Descent Start Time	Finish Time
Ascent Duration	Descent Duration	Total Time
Total Distance Covered	No. Of Steps

Companions

Weather

Enjoyment ◯◯◯◯◯◯◯◯◯◯
Views ◯◯◯◯◯◯◯◯◯◯
Difficulty ◯◯◯◯◯◯◯◯◯◯

Highlights

Notes

GREENLEIGHTON

Height (m): 285m
OS Grid Reference: NZ 03253 92186
Flush Bracket Number: S3622

Date	Parking ★★★★★	Map Ref: /60\
Ascent Start Time		Trig Time
Descent Start Time		Finish Time
Ascent Duration	Descent Duration	Total Time
Total Distance Covered		No. Of Steps

Companions

Weather

Enjoyment ○○○○○○○○○○
Views ○○○○○○○○○○
Difficulty ○○○○○○○○○○

Highlights

Notes

GREENSHEEN HILL

Height (m): 206m
OS Grid Reference: NU 05631 35758
Flush Bracket Number: S1616

Date	Parking ★ ★ ★ ★ ★	Map Ref: 61

Ascent Start Time	Trig Time

Descent Start Time	Finish Time

Ascent Duration	Descent Duration	Total Time

Total Distance Covered	No. Of Steps

Companions

Weather

- Enjoyment ○○○○○○○○○○
- Views ○○○○○○○○○○
- Difficulty ○○○○○○○○○○

Highlights

Notes

GREENSIDE

Height (m): 362m
OS Grid Reference: NY 63962 87708
Flush Bracket Number: S8081

Date	Parking	Map Ref: /62\

Ascent Start Time	Trig Time

Descent Start Time	Finish Time

Ascent Duration	Descent Duration	Total Time

Total Distance Covered	No. Of Steps

Companions

Weather

Enjoyment ○○○○○○○○○○
Views ○○○○○○○○○○
Difficulty ○○○○○○○○○○

Highlights

Notes

GREYS PIKE

Height (m): 446m
OS Grid Reference: NY 65547 93946
Flush Bracket Number: S7907

| Date | Parking ★★★★★ | Map Ref: 63 |

Ascent Start Time | **Trig Time**

Descent Start Time | **Finish Time**

Ascent Duration | **Descent Duration** | **Total Time**

Total Distance Covered | **No. Of Steps**

Companions

Weather

Enjoyment ○○○○○○○○○○
Views ○○○○○○○○○○
Difficulty ○○○○○○○○○○

Highlights

Notes

HALIDON HILL

Height (m): 163m
OS Grid Reference: NT 96866 54831
Flush Bracket Number: S6232

Date	Parking	Map Ref: 64
Ascent Start Time		Trig Time
Descent Start Time		Finish Time
Ascent Duration	Descent Duration	Total Time
Total Distance Covered		No. Of Steps

Companions

Weather

Enjoyment ○○○○○○○○○○
Views ○○○○○○○○○○
Difficulty ○○○○○○○○○○

Highlights

Notes

HANGWELL LAW

Height (m): 212m
OS Grid Reference: NU 12413 24467
Flush Bracket Number: S3577

| Date | Parking ☆☆☆☆☆ | Map Ref: /65\ |

Ascent Start Time | **Trig Time**

Descent Start Time | **Finish Time**

Ascent Duration | **Descent Duration** | **Total Time**

Total Distance Covered | **No. Of Steps**

Companions

Weather

Enjoyment ○○○○○○○○○○
Views   ○○○○○○○○○○
Difficulty ○○○○○○○○○○

Highlights

Notes

HARBOTTLE

Height (m): 361m
OS Grid Reference: NT 92332 03092
Flush Bracket Number: S8066

| Date | Parking | ☆☆☆☆☆ | Map Ref: /66\ |

Ascent Start Time | Trig Time

Descent Start Time | Finish Time

Ascent Duration | Descent Duration | Total Time

Total Distance Covered | No. Of Steps

Companions

Weather

Enjoyment ○○○○○○○○○○
Views   ○○○○○○○○○○
Difficulty ○○○○○○○○○○

Highlights

Notes

HARD RIGG

Height (m): 547m
OS Grid Reference: NY 74987 48759
Flush Bracket Number: S6493

| Date | Parking ★ ★ ★ ★ ★ | Map Ref: /67\ |

Ascent Start Time | Trig Time

Descent Start Time | Finish Time

Ascent Duration | Descent Duration | Total Time

Total Distance Covered | No. Of Steps

Companions

Weather

Enjoyment ○ ○ ○ ○ ○ ○ ○ ○ ○ ○
Views ○ ○ ○ ○ ○ ○ ○ ○ ○ ○
Difficulty ○ ○ ○ ○ ○ ○ ○ ○ ○ ○

Highlights

Notes

HART LAW

Height (m): 341m
OS Grid Reference: NT 98834 12818
Flush Bracket Number: S8034

Date	Parking	Map Ref: /68

Ascent Start Time | Trig Time

Descent Start Time | Finish Time

Ascent Duration | Descent Duration | Total Time

Total Distance Covered | No. Of Steps

Companions

Weather

Enjoyment ○ ○ ○ ○ ○ ○ ○ ○ ○ ○
Views ○ ○ ○ ○ ○ ○ ○ ○ ○ ○
Difficulty ○ ○ ○ ○ ○ ○ ○ ○ ○ ○

Highlights

Notes

HARWOOD SIDE

Height (m): 489m
OS Grid Reference: NY 86743 51447
Flush Bracket Number: S6657

Date	Parking ★★★★★	Map Ref: 69

Ascent Start Time | **Trig Time**

Descent Start Time | **Finish Time**

Ascent Duration | **Descent Duration** | **Total Time**

Total Distance Covered | **No. Of Steps**

Companions

Weather

Enjoyment ○○○○○○○○○○
Views ○○○○○○○○○○
Difficulty ○○○○○○○○○○

Highlights

Notes

HAYDON FELL

Height (m): 244m
OS Grid Reference: NY 84520 66807
Flush Bracket Number: S6661

Date	Parking	Map Ref: /70\

Ascent Start Time	Trig Time

Descent Start Time	Finish Time

Ascent Duration	Descent Duration	Total Time

Total Distance Covered	No. Of Steps

Companions

Weather

Enjoyment ○ ○ ○ ○ ○ ○ ○ ○ ○ ○
Views ○ ○ ○ ○ ○ ○ ○ ○ ○ ○
Difficulty ○ ○ ○ ○ ○ ○ ○ ○ ○ ○

Highlights

Notes

HEBRON HILL

Height (m): 130m
OS Grid Reference: NZ 18854 90358
Flush Bracket Number: S3685

Date	Parking ★★★★★	Map Ref: 71
Ascent Start Time		Trig Time
Descent Start Time		Finish Time
Ascent Duration	Descent Duration	Total Time
Total Distance Covered		No. Of Steps

Companions

Weather

Enjoyment ○○○○○○○○○○
Views ○○○○○○○○○○
Difficulty ○○○○○○○○○○

Highlights

Notes

HEDDON HILL

Height (m): 278m
OS Grid Reference: NU 00415 20300
Flush Bracket Number: S3566

Date	Parking ★★★★★	Map Ref: 72

Ascent Start Time | **Trig Time**

Descent Start Time | **Finish Time**

Ascent Duration | **Descent Duration** | **Total Time**

Total Distance Covered | **No. Of Steps**

Companions

Weather

Enjoyment ○○○○○○○○○○
Views ○○○○○○○○○○
Difficulty ○○○○○○○○○○

Highlights

Notes

HEDGEHOPE HILL

Height (m): 716m
OS Grid Reference: NT 94386 19790
Flush Bracket Number: S8059

Date	Parking ★★★★★	Map Ref: /73\
Ascent Start Time		Trig Time
Descent Start Time		Finish Time
Ascent Duration	Descent Duration	Total Time
Total Distance Covered		No. Of Steps

Companions

Weather

Enjoyment ○○○○○○○○○○
Views ○○○○○○○○○○
Difficulty ○○○○○○○○○○

Highlights

Notes

HEDLEY HILL

Height (m): 147m
OS Grid Reference: NZ 14303 96600
Flush Bracket Number: S3691

Date	Parking ☆☆☆☆☆	Map Ref: /74\

Ascent Start Time | **Trig Time**

Descent Start Time | **Finish Time**

Ascent Duration | **Descent Duration** | **Total Time**

Total Distance Covered | **No. Of Steps**

Companions

Weather

Enjoyment ○○○○○○○○○○
Views ○○○○○○○○○○
Difficulty ○○○○○○○○○○

Highlights

Notes

HELM

Height (m): 107m
OS Grid Reference: NZ 18849 96549
Flush Bracket Number: S3684

Date	Parking ★ ★ ★ ★ ★	Map Ref: /75\

Ascent Start Time — **Trig Time**

Descent Start Time — **Finish Time**

Ascent Duration — **Descent Duration** — **Total Time**

Total Distance Covered — **No. Of Steps**

Companions

Weather

Enjoyment ○○○○○○○○○○
Views ○○○○○○○○○○
Difficulty ○○○○○○○○○○

Highlights

Notes

HEXHAM COMMON

Height (m): 291m
OS Grid Reference: NY 88705 59873
Flush Bracket Number: S6495

Date		Parking	★ ★ ★ ★ ★	Map Ref:	76

Ascent Start Time | **Trig Time**

Descent Start Time | **Finish Time**

Ascent Duration | **Descent Duration** | **Total Time**

Total Distance Covered | **No. Of Steps**

Companions

Weather

Enjoyment ○ ○ ○ ○ ○ ○ ○ ○ ○ ○
Views ○ ○ ○ ○ ○ ○ ○ ○ ○ ○
Difficulty ○ ○ ○ ○ ○ ○ ○ ○ ○ ○

Highlights

Notes

HEXHAM RACECOURSE

Height (m): 233m
OS Grid Reference: NY 91879 62322
Flush Bracket Number: S6579

| Date | Parking ★★★★★ | Map Ref: 77 |

Ascent Start Time | Trig Time

Descent Start Time | Finish Time

Ascent Duration | Descent Duration | Total Time

Total Distance Covered | No. Of Steps

Companions

Weather

Enjoyment ○○○○○○○○○
Views ○○○○○○○○○
Difficulty ○○○○○○○○○

Highlights

Notes

HIGH TREWHITT

Height (m): 165m
OS Grid Reference: NU 01133 05215
Flush Bracket Number: S3548

Date	Parking	Map Ref: /78\

| Ascent Start Time | | Trig Time | |

| Descent Start Time | | Finish Time | |

| Ascent Duration | Descent Duration | Total Time |

| Total Distance Covered | | No. Of Steps |

Companions

Weather

Enjoyment ○ ○ ○ ○ ○ ○ ○ ○ ○ ○
Views ○ ○ ○ ○ ○ ○ ○ ○ ○ ○
Difficulty ○ ○ ○ ○ ○ ○ ○ ○ ○ ○

Highlights

Notes

HIGHFIELD

Height (m): 309m
OS Grid Reference: NY 74790 88176
Flush Bracket Number: S8082

Date	Parking ☆☆☆☆☆	Map Ref: /79\

Ascent Start Time | **Trig Time**

Descent Start Time | **Finish Time**

Ascent Duration | **Descent Duration** | **Total Time**

Total Distance Covered | **No. Of Steps**

Companions

Weather

Enjoyment ○○○○○○○○○○
Views ○○○○○○○○○○
Difficulty ○○○○○○○○○○

Highlights

Notes

HILLHEAD

Height (m): 171m
OS Grid Reference: NU 19100 08028
Flush Bracket Number: S3690

Date	Parking ★★★★★	Map Ref: /80\

Ascent Start Time	Trig Time

Descent Start Time	Finish Time

Ascent Duration	Descent Duration	Total Time

Total Distance Covered	No. Of Steps

Companions

Weather

Enjoyment ○○○○○○○○○○
Views ○○○○○○○○○○
Difficulty ○○○○○○○○○○

Highlights

Notes

HINDHOPE LAW

Height (m): 426m
OS Grid Reference: NY 76711 97432
Flush Bracket Number: S8070

Date	Parking ★★★★★	Map Ref: /81\
Ascent Start Time		Trig Time
Descent Start Time		Finish Time
Ascent Duration	Descent Duration	Total Time
Total Distance Covered		No. Of Steps

Companions

Weather

- Enjoyment ○○○○○○○○○○
- Views ○○○○○○○○○○
- Difficulty ○○○○○○○○○○

Highlights

Notes

HIPS HEUGH

Height (m): 58m
OS Grid Reference: NU 25219 18430
Flush Bracket Number: S3569

Date	Parking	Map Ref: 82
Ascent Start Time		Trig Time
Descent Start Time		Finish Time
Ascent Duration	Descent Duration	Total Time
Total Distance Covered		No. Of Steps
Companions		

Weather

Enjoyment ○ ○ ○ ○ ○ ○ ○ ○ ○ ○
Views ○ ○ ○ ○ ○ ○ ○ ○ ○ ○
Difficulty ○ ○ ○ ○ ○ ○ ○ ○ ○ ○

Highlights

Notes

HOPEALONE

Height (m): 316m
OS Grid Reference: NY 74080 72018
Flush Bracket Number: S6499

| Date | Parking ★ ★ ★ ★ ★ | Map Ref: 83 |

Ascent Start Time | **Trig Time**

Descent Start Time | **Finish Time**

Ascent Duration | **Descent Duration** | **Total Time**

Total Distance Covered | **No. Of Steps**

Companions

Weather

Enjoyment ○○○○○○○○○○
Views ○○○○○○○○○○
Difficulty ○○○○○○○○○○

Highlights

Notes

HUNGRY LAW

Height (m): 501m
OS Grid Reference: NT 74718 06142
Flush Bracket Number: S7912

Date	Parking ★ ★ ★ ★ ★	Map Ref: /84\

Ascent Start Time	Trig Time

Descent Start Time	Finish Time

Ascent Duration	Descent Duration	Total Time

Total Distance Covered	No. Of Steps

Companions

Weather

Enjoyment ○ ○ ○ ○ ○ ○ ○ ○ ○ ○
Views ○ ○ ○ ○ ○ ○ ○ ○ ○ ○
Difficulty ○ ○ ○ ○ ○ ○ ○ ○ ○ ○

Highlights

Notes

KILLHOPE LAW

Height (m): 673m
OS Grid Reference: NY 81948 44858
Flush Bracket Number: S6664

| Date | Parking ★★★★★ | Map Ref: /85 |

Ascent Start Time | Trig Time

Descent Start Time | Finish Time

Ascent Duration | Descent Duration | Total Time

Total Distance Covered | No. Of Steps

Companions

Weather

Enjoyment ○○○○○○○○○○
Views ○○○○○○○○○○
Difficulty ○○○○○○○○○○

Highlights

Notes

KINGS SEAT

Height (m): 532m
OS Grid Reference: NT 87886 17344
Flush Bracket Number: S7997

Date	Parking ★★★★★	Map Ref: /86\

Ascent Start Time	Trig Time

Descent Start Time	Finish Time

Ascent Duration	Descent Duration	Total Time

Total Distance Covered	No. Of Steps

Companions

Weather

Enjoyment ○○○○○○○○○○
Views ○○○○○○○○○○
Difficulty ○○○○○○○○○○

Highlights

Notes

LAMB HILL

Height (m): 511m
OS Grid Reference: NT 81059 13337
Flush Bracket Number: S7989

Date	Parking ★★★★★	Map Ref: 87
Ascent Start Time	Trig Time	
Descent Start Time	Finish Time	
Ascent Duration	Descent Duration	Total Time
Total Distance Covered		No. Of Steps

Companions

Weather

- Enjoyment ○○○○○○○○○○
- Views ○○○○○○○○○○
- Difficulty ○○○○○○○○○○

Highlights

Notes

LANE END

Height (m): 143m
OS Grid Reference: NU 06958 11059
Flush Bracket Number: S3570

Date	Parking ★★★★★	Map Ref: /88\

Ascent Start Time — Trig Time

Descent Start Time — Finish Time

Ascent Duration — **Descent Duration** — **Total Time**

Total Distance Covered — No. Of Steps

Companions

Weather

Enjoyment ○○○○○○○○○○
Views ○○○○○○○○○○
Difficulty ○○○○○○○○○○

Highlights

Notes

LAW PLANTATION

Height (m): 177m
OS Grid Reference: NU 11219 30479
Flush Bracket Number: S3567

| Date | Parking ⭐⭐⭐⭐⭐ | Map Ref: /89\ |

Ascent Start Time | Trig Time

Descent Start Time | Finish Time

Ascent Duration | Descent Duration | Total Time

Total Distance Covered | No. Of Steps

Companions

Weather

Enjoyment ○○○○○○○○○
Views ○○○○○○○○○
Difficulty ○○○○○○○○○

Highlights

Notes

LIMESTONE BANK

Height (m): 251m
OS Grid Reference: NY 87783 71551
Flush Bracket Number: S6659

Date	Parking ★★★★★	Map Ref: /90\
Ascent Start Time		Trig Time
Descent Start Time		Finish Time
Ascent Duration	Descent Duration	Total Time
Total Distance Covered		No. Of Steps
Companions		
Weather		

Enjoyment ○○○○○○○○○○
Views ○○○○○○○○○○
Difficulty ○○○○○○○○○○

Highlights

Notes

LINBRIG

Height (m): 390m
OS Grid Reference: NT 90299 07313
Flush Bracket Number: S8058

| Date | Parking | Map Ref: /91 |

Ascent Start Time | Trig Time

Descent Start Time | Finish Time

Ascent Duration | Descent Duration | Total Time

Total Distance Covered | No. Of Steps

Companions

Weather

Enjoyment
Views
Difficulty

Highlights

Notes

LONG CRAG

Height (m): 320m
OS Grid Reference: NU 06223 06934
Flush Bracket Number: S3572

Date	Parking ★★★★★	Map Ref: /92\

Ascent Start Time	Trig Time

Descent Start Time	Finish Time

Ascent Duration	Descent Duration	Total Time

Total Distance Covered	No. Of Steps

Companions

Weather

Enjoyment ○○○○○○○○○○
Views ○○○○○○○○○○
Difficulty ○○○○○○○○○○

Highlights

Notes

LONG CRAG GUNNERTON

Height (m): 222m
OS Grid Reference: NY 92266 77755
Flush Bracket Number: S6625

Date	Parking ★★★★★	Map Ref: 93
Ascent Start Time		Trig Time
Descent Start Time		Finish Time
Ascent Duration	Descent Duration	Total Time
Total Distance Covered		No. Of Steps
Companions		

Weather

- Enjoyment ○○○○○○○○○○
- Views ○○○○○○○○○○
- Difficulty ○○○○○○○○○○

Highlights

Notes

LONGKNOWE HILL

Height (m): 346m
OS Grid Reference: NT 87470 30144
Flush Bracket Number: S7436

Date	Parking ★★★★★	Map Ref: /94\

Ascent Start Time	Trig Time

Descent Start Time	Finish Time

Ascent Duration	Descent Duration	Total Time

Total Distance Covered	No. Of Steps

Companions

Weather

Enjoyment ○ ○ ○ ○ ○ ○ ○ ○ ○ ○
Views ○ ○ ○ ○ ○ ○ ○ ○ ○ ○
Difficulty ○ ○ ○ ○ ○ ○ ○ ○ ○ ○

Highlights

Notes

MANSIDE CROSS

Height (m): 325m
OS Grid Reference: NY 98388 92063
Flush Bracket Number: S3625

Date	Parking ☆☆☆☆☆	Map Ref: /95\

Ascent Start Time | **Trig Time**

Descent Start Time | **Finish Time**

Ascent Duration | **Descent Duration** | **Total Time**

Total Distance Covered | **No. Of Steps**

Companions

Weather

Enjoyment ○○○○○○○○○○
Views ○○○○○○○○○○
Difficulty ○○○○○○○○○○

Highlights

Notes

MARCH HEAD

Height (m): 454m
OS Grid Reference: NY 60569 91945
Flush Bracket Number: S8000

Date	Parking	Map Ref: /96\
Ascent Start Time		Trig Time
Descent Start Time		Finish Time
Ascent Duration	Descent Duration	Total Time
Total Distance Covered		No. Of Steps
Companions		
Weather		

Enjoyment ○○○○○○○○○○
Views ○○○○○○○○○○
Difficulty ○○○○○○○○○○

Highlights

Notes

MATTILEES HILL

Height (m): 109m
OS Grid Reference: NT 94010 43457
Flush Bracket Number: S6459

Date	Parking ☆☆☆☆☆	Map Ref: 97

Ascent Start Time — **Trig Time**

Descent Start Time — **Finish Time**

Ascent Duration — **Descent Duration** — **Total Time**

Total Distance Covered — **No. Of Steps**

Companions

Weather

Enjoyment ○○○○○○○○○○
Views ○○○○○○○○○○
Difficulty ○○○○○○○○○○

Highlights

Notes

MENCELES

Height (m): 78m
OS Grid Reference: NU 04744 21909
Flush Bracket Number: S3554

| Date | Parking ★★★★★ | Map Ref: /98\ |

Ascent Start Time | Trig Time

Descent Start Time | Finish Time

Ascent Duration | Descent Duration | Total Time

Total Distance Covered | No. Of Steps

Companions

Weather

Enjoyment ○○○○○○○○○○
Views ○○○○○○○○○○
Difficulty ○○○○○○○○○○

Highlights

Notes

MIDHOPELAW PIKE

Height (m): 326m
OS Grid Reference: NY 82401 87118
Flush Bracket Number: S6628

Date	Parking ★★★★★	Map Ref: /99\

Ascent Start Time | **Trig Time**

Descent Start Time | **Finish Time**

Ascent Duration | **Descent Duration** | **Total Time**

Total Distance Covered | **No. Of Steps**

Companions

Weather

Enjoyment ○○○○○○○○○○
Views ○○○○○○○○○○
Difficulty ○○○○○○○○○○

Highlights

Notes

MILITARY ROAD

Height (m): 269m
OS Grid Reference: NY 97315 68989
Flush Bracket Number: S6623

Date	Parking ★★★★★	Map Ref: /100
Ascent Start Time		Trig Time
Descent Start Time		Finish Time
Ascent Duration	Descent Duration	Total Time
Total Distance Covered		No. Of Steps
Companions		

Weather

Enjoyment ◯◯◯◯◯◯◯◯◯◯
Views   ◯◯◯◯◯◯◯◯◯◯
Difficulty ◯◯◯◯◯◯◯◯◯◯

Highlights

Notes

MONKSIDE

Height (m): 513m
OS Grid Reference: NY 68505 94985
Flush Bracket Number: S7992

| Date | Parking ★★★★★ | Map Ref: /101\ |

Ascent Start Time | **Trig Time**

Descent Start Time | **Finish Time**

Ascent Duration | **Descent Duration** | **Total Time**

Total Distance Covered | **No. Of Steps**

Companions

Weather

Enjoyment ◯◯◯◯◯◯◯◯◯◯
Views ◯◯◯◯◯◯◯◯◯◯
Difficulty ◯◯◯◯◯◯◯◯◯◯

Highlights

Notes

MONYLAWS

Height (m): 246m
OS Grid Reference: NT 87249 34731
Flush Bracket Number: S7385

| Date | Parking ★★★★★ | Map Ref: 102 |

Ascent Start Time | Trig Time

Descent Start Time | Finish Time

Ascent Duration | Descent Duration | Total Time

Total Distance Covered | No. Of Steps

Companions

Weather

Enjoyment ○○○○○○○○○○
Views ○○○○○○○○○○
Difficulty ○○○○○○○○○○

Highlights

Notes

MOOT LAW

Height (m): 258m
OS Grid Reference: NZ 01073 75960
Flush Bracket Number: S3995

Date	Parking	Map Ref: /103\

- Ascent Start Time
- Trig Time
- Descent Start Time
- Finish Time
- Ascent Duration
- Descent Duration
- Total Time
- Total Distance Covered
- No. Of Steps
- Companions

Weather

- Enjoyment
- Views
- Difficulty

Highlights

Notes

MURTON WHITEHOUSE

Height (m): 109m
OS Grid Reference: NT 97979 49527
Flush Bracket Number: S7231

Date	Parking	Map Ref: 104

Ascent Start Time	Trig Time

Descent Start Time	Finish Time

Ascent Duration	Descent Duration	Total Time

Total Distance Covered	No. Of Steps

Companions

Weather

Enjoyment ◯ ◯ ◯ ◯ ◯ ◯ ◯ ◯ ◯ ◯
Views   ◯ ◯ ◯ ◯ ◯ ◯ ◯ ◯ ◯ ◯
Difficulty ◯ ◯ ◯ ◯ ◯ ◯ ◯ ◯ ◯ ◯

Highlights

Notes

NEW HEATON

Height (m): 92m
OS Grid Reference: NT 88452 40630
Flush Bracket Number: S7391

✓

Date	29.5.2022	Parking	★★★✓★
Ascent Start Time	11:10am	Trig Time	12pm
Descent Start Time	12:15pm	Finish Time	1pm
Ascent Duration		Descent Duration	Total Time
Total Distance Covered		No. Of Steps	8110

Map Ref: /105\

Companions: Sienna, Lucia, Mario + Lucy

Weather:

Enjoyment: ○○○○○○✓○
Views: ○○○○○✓○○
Difficulty: ○○✓○○○○○

Highlights: Lucy catching a partridge and bringing it over to us. Our first ever trig point in the book :)

Notes: Cramondhill is nearby but need to go back in autumn when no crops in field.

NEWTON TORS

Height (m): 537m
OS Grid Reference: NT 90812 26924
Flush Bracket Number: S7473

Map Ref: 106

Date	Parking	★ ★ ★ ★ ★
Ascent Start Time		Trig Time
Descent Start Time		Finish Time
Ascent Duration	Descent Duration	Total Time
Total Distance Covered		No. Of Steps
Companions		
Weather		

Enjoyment ○ ○ ○ ○ ○ ○ ○ ○ ○ ○
Views ○ ○ ○ ○ ○ ○ ○ ○ ○ ○
Difficulty ○ ○ ○ ○ ○ ○ ○ ○ ○ ○

Highlights

Notes

NIGHT FOLD FIELD

Height (m): 48m
OS Grid Reference: NU 24786 10949
Flush Bracket Number: S3689

Date	Parking	Map Ref: /107\

Ascent Start Time | Trig Time

Descent Start Time | Finish Time

Ascent Duration | Descent Duration | Total Time

Total Distance Covered | No. Of Steps

Companions

Weather

Enjoyment
Views
Difficulty

Highlights

Notes

OLD FAWDON HILL

Height (m): 315m
OS Grid Reference: NU 02253 14143
Flush Bracket Number: S2349

Date	Parking ★★★★★	Map Ref: /108\
Ascent Start Time		Trig Time
Descent Start Time		Finish Time
Ascent Duration	Descent Duration	Total Time
Total Distance Covered		No. Of Steps

Companions

Weather

Enjoytment ○○○○○○○○○○
Views   ○○○○○○○○○○
Difficulty ○○○○○○○○○○

Highlights

Notes

PASTURE HILL PLANTATION

Height (m): 95m
OS Grid Reference: NU 20366 19832
Flush Bracket Number: S3553

Date	Parking ★★★★★	Map Ref: 109

Ascent Start Time | **Trig Time**

Descent Start Time | **Finish Time**

Ascent Duration | **Descent Duration** | **Total Time**

Total Distance Covered | **No. Of Steps**

Companions

Weather

Enjoyment ○○○○○○○○○○
Views ○○○○○○○○○○
Difficulty ○○○○○○○○○○

Highlights

Notes

PIGDON

Height (m): 118m
OS Grid Reference: NZ 14791 88211
Flush Bracket Number: S3686

Date	Parking ★★★★★	Map Ref: 110

Ascent Start Time	Trig Time

Descent Start Time	Finish Time

Ascent Duration	Descent Duration	Total Time

Total Distance Covered	No. Of Steps

Companions

Weather

Enjoyment ○○○○○○○○○○
Views ○○○○○○○○○○
Difficulty ○○○○○○○○○○

Highlights

Notes

PIKE RIGG

Height (m): 525m
OS Grid Reference: NY 72989 53945
Flush Bracket Number: S6663

Date	Parking ★★★★★	Map Ref: /111\
Ascent Start Time		Trig Time
Descent Start Time		Finish Time
Ascent Duration	Descent Duration	Total Time
Total Distance Covered		No. Of Steps
Companions		
Weather		

- Enjoyment ○○○○○○○○○○
- Views ○○○○○○○○○○
- Difficulty ○○○○○○○○○○

Highlights

Notes

RAVENSHEUGH CRAGS

Height (m): 256m
OS Grid Reference: NY 83164 74858
Flush Bracket Number: S6622

Date	Parking ★★★★★	Map Ref: /112\
Ascent Start Time		Trig Time
Descent Start Time		Finish Time
Ascent Duration	Descent Duration	Total Time
Total Distance Covered		No. Of Steps
Companions		
Weather		

Enjoyment ○○○○○○○○○○
Views ○○○○○○○○○○
Difficulty ○○○○○○○○○○

Highlights

Notes

REAVELEY HILL

Height (m): 302m
OS Grid Reference: NT 99776 17679
Flush Bracket Number: S8032

Date	Parking ☆☆☆☆☆	Map Ref: /113\

Ascent Start Time | **Trig Time**

Descent Start Time | **Finish Time**

Ascent Duration | **Descent Duration** | **Total Time**

Total Distance Covered | **No. Of Steps**

Companions

Weather

Enjoyment ○○○○○○○○○○
Views ○○○○○○○○○○
Difficulty ○○○○○○○○○○

Highlights

Notes

RHODES HILL

Height (m): 146m
OS Grid Reference: NT 94499 40087
Flush Bracket Number: S7384

| Date | Parking ★★★★★ | Map Ref: 114 |

Ascent Start Time | **Trig Time**

Descent Start Time | **Finish Time**

Ascent Duration | **Descent Duration** | **Total Time**

Total Distance Covered | **No. Of Steps**

Companions

Weather

- Enjoyment ○○○○○○○○○○
- Views ○○○○○○○○○○
- Difficulty ○○○○○○○○○○

Highlights

Notes

RIDLEES CAIRN

Height (m): 412m
OS Grid Reference: NT 84049 04262
Flush Bracket Number: S7427

Date	Parking ★ ★ ★ ★ ★	Map Ref: 115

Ascent Start Time | **Trig Time**

Descent Start Time | **Finish Time**

Ascent Duration | **Descent Duration** | **Total Time**

Total Distance Covered | **No. Of Steps**

Companions

Weather

Enjoyment ○ ○ ○ ○ ○ ○ ○ ○ ○ ○
Views ○ ○ ○ ○ ○ ○ ○ ○ ○ ○
Difficulty ○ ○ ○ ○ ○ ○ ○ ○ ○ ○

Highlights

Notes

RIPLEY CARRS

Height (m): 438m
OS Grid Reference: NY 79839 54207
Flush Bracket Number: S6656

Date	Parking	Map Ref: /116\

Ascent Start Time | Trig Time

Descent Start Time | Finish Time

Ascent Duration | Descent Duration | Total Time

Total Distance Covered | No. Of Steps

Companions

Weather

Enjoyment
Views
Difficulty

Highlights

Notes

ROSS CASTLE

Height (m): 316m
OS Grid Reference: NU 08112 25327
Flush Bracket Number: S3697

| Date | Parking ★★★★★ | Map Ref: 117 |

Ascent Start Time | **Trig Time**

Descent Start Time | **Finish Time**

Ascent Duration | **Descent Duration** | **Total Time**

Total Distance Covered | **No. Of Steps**

Companions

Weather

Enjoyment ○○○○○○○○○○
Views ○○○○○○○○○○
Difficulty ○○○○○○○○○○

Highlights

Notes

ROUND TOP

Height (m): 325m
OS Grid Reference: NY 71697 76646
Flush Bracket Number: S6496

Date	Parking ★★★★★	Map Ref: /118\
Ascent Start Time		Trig Time
Descent Start Time		Finish Time
Ascent Duration	Descent Duration	Total Time
Total Distance Covered		No. Of Steps
Companions		
Weather		

Enjoyment ○○○○○○○○○○
Views ○○○○○○○○○○
Difficulty ○○○○○○○○○○

Highlights

Notes

SEWINGSHIELDS CRAGS

Height (m): 326m
OS Grid Reference: NY 80021 70047
Flush Bracket Number: S6653

Date	Parking	Map Ref: 119

Ascent Start Time | **Trig Time**

Descent Start Time | **Finish Time**

Ascent Duration | **Descent Duration** | **Total Time**

Total Distance Covered | **No. Of Steps**

Companions

Weather

- Enjoyment ○○○○○○○○○○
- Views ○○○○○○○○○○
- Difficulty ○○○○○○○○○○

Highlights

Notes

SHAFTOE CRAGS

Height (m): 213m
OS Grid Reference: NZ 05103 81887
Flush Bracket Number: S3707

Date	Parking	Map Ref: /120\

| Ascent Start Time | | Trig Time | |

| Descent Start Time | | Finish Time | |

| Ascent Duration | Descent Duration | Total Time |

| Total Distance Covered | | No. Of Steps | |

Companions

Weather

- Enjoyment ○ ○ ○ ○ ○ ○ ○ ○ ○ ○
- Views ○ ○ ○ ○ ○ ○ ○ ○ ○ ○
- Difficulty ○ ○ ○ ○ ○ ○ ○ ○ ○ ○

Highlights

Notes

SHEPHERDSKIRK HILL

Height (m): 202m
OS Grid Reference: NU 04558 38341
Flush Bracket Number: S7009

Date

Parking ★ ★ ★ ★ ★

Map Ref: 121

Ascent Start Time

Trig Time

Descent Start Time

Finish Time

Ascent Duration

Descent Duration

Total Time

Total Distance Covered

No. Of Steps

Companions

Weather

Enjoyment ○ ○ ○ ○ ○ ○ ○ ○ ○ ○
Views ○ ○ ○ ○ ○ ○ ○ ○ ○ ○
Difficulty ○ ○ ○ ○ ○ ○ ○ ○ ○ ○

Highlights

Notes

SHILL MOOR

Height (m): 529m
OS Grid Reference: NT 94397 15311
Flush Bracket Number: S7991

Date	Parking	Map Ref: 122
Ascent Start Time		Trig Time
Descent Start Time		Finish Time
Ascent Duration	Descent Duration	Total Time
Total Distance Covered		No. Of Steps

Companions

Weather

Enjoyment
Views
Difficulty

Highlights

Notes

SHILLHOPE LAW

Height (m): 501m
OS Grid Reference: NT 87310 09677
Flush Bracket Number: S8079

Date	Parking ★ ★ ★ ★ ★	Map Ref: /123\

Ascent Start Time | **Trig Time**

Descent Start Time | **Finish Time**

Ascent Duration | **Descent Duration** | **Total Time**

Total Distance Covered | **No. Of Steps**

Companions

Weather

Enjoyment ○ ○ ○ ○ ○ ○ ○ ○ ○ ○
Views ○ ○ ○ ○ ○ ○ ○ ○ ○ ○
Difficulty ○ ○ ○ ○ ○ ○ ○ ○ ○ ○

Highlights

Notes

SHORESWOOD

Height (m): 92m
OS Grid Reference: NT 93550 46271
Flush Bracket Number: S6461

Date	Parking ☆☆☆☆☆	Map Ref: /124\
Ascent Start Time		Trig Time
Descent Start Time		Finish Time
Ascent Duration	Descent Duration	Total Time
Total Distance Covered		No. Of Steps
Companions		

Weather

Enjoyment ○○○○○○○○○○
Views ○○○○○○○○○○
Difficulty ○○○○○○○○○○

Highlights

Notes

SPY RIGG

Height (m): 313m
OS Grid Reference: NY 68885 75859
Flush Bracket Number: S6490

Date	Parking ★★★★★	Map Ref: /125\
Ascent Start Time		Trig Time
Descent Start Time		Finish Time
Ascent Duration	Descent Duration	Total Time
Total Distance Covered		No. Of Steps
Companions		

Weather

Enjoment ○○○○○○○○○○
Views ○○○○○○○○○○
Difficulty ○○○○○○○○○○

Highlights

Notes

STOKOE HIGH CRAGS

Height (m): 230m
OS Grid Reference: NY 75061 84804
Flush Bracket Number: S6560

Date	Parking ★ ★ ★ ★ ★	Map Ref: 126
Ascent Start Time		Trig Time
Descent Start Time		Finish Time
Ascent Duration	Descent Duration	Total Time
Total Distance Covered		No. Of Steps

Companions

Weather

Enjoyment ○ ○ ○ ○ ○ ○ ○ ○ ○ ○
Views ○ ○ ○ ○ ○ ○ ○ ○ ○ ○
Difficulty ○ ○ ○ ○ ○ ○ ○ ○ ○ ○

Highlights

Notes

TARGET PLANTATION

Height (m): 250m
OS Grid Reference: NU 04695 02774
Flush Bracket Number: S3547

| Date | Parking ★★★★★ | Map Ref: /127\ |

Ascent Start Time | **Trig Time**

Descent Start Time | **Finish Time**

Ascent Duration | **Descent Duration** | **Total Time**

Total Distance Covered | **No. Of Steps**

Companions

Weather

Enjoyment ○○○○○○○○○○
Views ○○○○○○○○○○
Difficulty ○○○○○○○○○○

Highlights

Notes

THE BEACON

Height (m): 301m
OS Grid Reference: NT 95507 00276
Flush Bracket Number: S8062

Date	Parking ★★★★★	Map Ref: /128\

Ascent Start Time	Trig Time

Descent Start Time	Finish Time

Ascent Duration	Descent Duration	Total Time

Total Distance Covered	No. Of Steps

Companions

Weather

Enjoyment ○ ○ ○ ○ ○ ○ ○ ○ ○ ○
Views   ○ ○ ○ ○ ○ ○ ○ ○ ○ ○
Difficulty ○ ○ ○ ○ ○ ○ ○ ○ ○ ○

Highlights

Notes

THE DODD

Height (m): 354m
OS Grid Reference: NY 73509 92542
Flush Bracket Number: S8064

Date	Parking	Map Ref: 129

Ascent Start Time | **Trig Time**

Descent Start Time | **Finish Time**

Ascent Duration | **Descent Duration** | **Total Time**

Total Distance Covered | **No. Of Steps**

Companions

Weather

- Enjoyment
- Views
- Difficulty

Highlights

Notes

THE GRUN

Height (m): 516m
OS Grid Reference: NT 66658 00344
Flush Bracket Number: S7909

Date	Parking	Map Ref: /130\

Ascent Start Time	Trig Time

Descent Start Time	Finish Time

Ascent Duration	Descent Duration	Total Time

Total Distance Covered	No. Of Steps

Companions

Weather

Enjoyment ○○○○○○○○○○
Views ○○○○○○○○○○
Difficulty ○○○○○○○○○○

Highlights

Notes

THIRL MOOR

Height (m): 558m
OS Grid Reference: NT 80593 08362
Flush Bracket Number: S7429

Date	Parking ★★★★★	Map Ref: /131\

Ascent Start Time	Trig Time

Descent Start Time	Finish Time

Ascent Duration	Descent Duration	Total Time

Total Distance Covered	No. Of Steps

Companions

Weather

Enjoyment ○○○○○○○○○○
Views ○○○○○○○○○○
Difficulty ○○○○○○○○○○

Highlights

Notes

THORNTON HOUSE

Height (m): 156m
OS Grid Reference: NZ 10022 86760
Flush Bracket Number: S3688

Date	Parking ☆☆☆☆☆	Map Ref: /132\

| Ascent Start Time | | Trig Time | |

| Descent Start Time | | Finish Time | |

| Ascent Duration | Descent Duration | Total Time |

| Total Distance Covered | | No. Of Steps |

Companions

Weather

Enjoyment ○○○○○○○○○○
Views ○○○○○○○○○○
Difficulty ○○○○○○○○○○

Highlights

Notes

THORNY HILL

Height (m): 185m
OS Grid Reference: NU 10034 00818
Flush Bracket Number: S3699

Date	Parking ★★★★★	Map Ref: /133\

Ascent Start Time	Trig Time

Descent Start Time	Finish Time

Ascent Duration	Descent Duration	Total Time

Total Distance Covered	No. Of Steps

Companions

Weather

Enjoyment ○○○○○○○○○○
Views ○○○○○○○○○○
Difficulty ○○○○○○○○○○

Highlights

Notes

TINELY MOOR

Height (m): 151m
OS Grid Reference: NU 16202 23665
Flush Bracket Number: S3576

Date	Parking ☆☆☆☆☆	Map Ref: /134\
Ascent Start Time		Trig Time
Descent Start Time		Finish Time
Ascent Duration	Descent Duration	Total Time
Total Distance Covered		No. Of Steps

Companions

Weather

Enjoncement ○○○○○○○○○○
Views ○○○○○○○○○○
Difficulty ○○○○○○○○○○

Highlights

Notes

TITLINGTON PIKE

Height (m): 233m
OS Grid Reference: NU 08751 15996
Flush Bracket Number: S3556

Date	Parking ★★★★★	Map Ref: /135\

Ascent Start Time — **Trig Time**

Descent Start Time — **Finish Time**

Ascent Duration — **Descent Duration** — **Total Time**

Total Distance Covered — **No. Of Steps**

Companions

Weather

Enjoyment ◯◯◯◯◯◯◯◯◯◯
Views   ◯◯◯◯◯◯◯◯◯◯
Difficulty ◯◯◯◯◯◯◯◯◯◯

Highlights

Notes

TOSSON HILL

Height (m): 442m
OS Grid Reference: NZ 00482 98246
Flush Bracket Number: S1551

Date	Parking ☆☆☆☆☆	Map Ref: /136\

Ascent Start Time	Trig Time

Descent Start Time	Finish Time

Ascent Duration	Descent Duration	Total Time

Total Distance Covered	No. Of Steps

Companions

Weather

Enjoyment ○○○○○○○○○○
Views ○○○○○○○○○○
Difficulty ○○○○○○○○○○

Highlights

Notes

WARDEN HILL

Height (m): 180m
OS Grid Reference: NY 90475 67824
Flush Bracket Number: S6662

Date	Parking ★★★★★	Map Ref: /137\
Ascent Start Time		Trig Time
Descent Start Time		Finish Time
Ascent Duration	Descent Duration	Total Time
Total Distance Covered		No. Of Steps
Companions		
Weather		

Enjoyment ○○○○○○○○○○
Views ○○○○○○○○○○
Difficulty ○○○○○○○○○○

Highlights

Notes

WARLAW PIKE

Height (m): 402m
OS Grid Reference: NY 94568 53469
Flush Bracket Number: S6701

Date	Parking ☆☆☆☆☆	Map Ref: /138\
Ascent Start Time		Trig Time
Descent Start Time		Finish Time
Ascent Duration	Descent Duration	Total Time
Total Distance Covered		No. Of Steps

Companions

Weather

Enjoyment ○○○○○○○○○○
Views ○○○○○○○○○○
Difficulty ○○○○○○○○○○

Highlights

Notes

WATCH CRAGS

Height (m): 291m
OS Grid Reference: NY 78676 82071
Flush Bracket Number: S6615

Date	Parking ★ ★ ★ ★ ★	Map Ref: 139
Ascent Start Time		Trig Time
Descent Start Time		Finish Time
Ascent Duration	Descent Duration	Total Time
Total Distance Covered		No. Of Steps
Companions		
Weather		

Enjoyment ○○○○○○○○○○
Views ○○○○○○○○○○
Difficulty ○○○○○○○○○○

Highlights

Notes

WATSONS PIKE

Height (m): 447m
OS Grid Reference: NY 89152 52788
Flush Bracket Number: S6700

Date	Parking ★★★★★	Map Ref: /140\

Ascent Start Time | **Trig Time**

Descent Start Time | **Finish Time**

Ascent Duration | **Descent Duration** | **Total Time**

Total Distance Covered | **No. Of Steps**

Companions

Weather

Enjoyment ○○○○○○○○○○
Views ○○○○○○○○○○
Difficulty ○○○○○○○○○○

Highlights

Notes

WETHER CAIRN

Height (m): 563m
OS Grid Reference: NT 94079 11626
Flush Bracket Number: S7994

Date	Parking ★★★★★	Map Ref: /141\

Ascent Start Time		Trig Time	

Descent Start Time		Finish Time	

Ascent Duration	Descent Duration	Total Time

Total Distance Covered	No. Of Steps

Companions

Weather

Enjoyment ○○○○○○○○○○
Views ○○○○○○○○○○
Difficulty ○○○○○○○○○○

Highlights

Notes

WETHER HILL

Height (m): 301m
OS Grid Reference: NY 92027 90295
Flush Bracket Number: S6724

Date	Parking ☆☆☆☆☆	Map Ref: /142\

Ascent Start Time		Trig Time	
Descent Start Time		Finish Time	
Ascent Duration	Descent Duration		Total Time
Total Distance Covered			No. Of Steps

Companions

Weather

Enjoyment ○○○○○○○○○○
Views ○○○○○○○○○○
Difficulty ○○○○○○○○○○

Highlights

Notes

WHITE CRAGS

Height (m): 537m
OS Grid Reference: NT 69768 01769
Flush Bracket Number: S7503

Date	Parking ★★★★★	Map Ref: /143\
Ascent Start Time		Trig Time
Descent Start Time		Finish Time
Ascent Duration	Descent Duration	Total Time
Total Distance Covered		No. Of Steps
Companions		

Weather

- Enjoyment ○○○○○○○○○○
- Views ○○○○○○○○○○
- Difficulty ○○○○○○○○○○

Highlights

Notes

WHITE HOUSE HILL

Height (m): 169m
OS Grid Reference: NU 16126 17829
Flush Bracket Number: S3534

Date	Parking ★★★★★	Map Ref: /144\

Ascent Start Time	Trig Time

Descent Start Time	Finish Time

Ascent Duration	Descent Duration	Total Time

Total Distance Covered	No. Of Steps

Companions

Weather

Enjoyment ○ ○ ○ ○ ○ ○ ○ ○ ○ ○
Views   ○ ○ ○ ○ ○ ○ ○ ○ ○ ○
Difficulty ○ ○ ○ ○ ○ ○ ○ ○ ○ ○

Highlights

Notes

WHITEHILL

Height (m): 247m
OS Grid Reference: NY 99373 85646
Flush Bracket Number: S3624

| Date | Parking ★ ★ ★ ★ ★ | Map Ref: /145\ |

Ascent Start Time	Trig Time
Descent Start Time	Finish Time
Ascent Duration	Descent Duration	Total Time
Total Distance Covered	No. Of Steps

Companions

Weather

Enjoyment ○ ○ ○ ○ ○ ○ ○ ○ ○ ○
Views ○ ○ ○ ○ ○ ○ ○ ○ ○ ○
Difficulty ○ ○ ○ ○ ○ ○ ○ ○ ○ ○

Highlights

Notes

WHITSUNBANK HILL

Height (m): 167m
OS Grid Reference: NU 01572 27663
Flush Bracket Number: S3584

| Date | Parking ☆☆☆☆☆ | Map Ref: /146\ |
|---|---|---|//
Ascent Start Time		Trig Time
Descent Start Time		Finish Time
Ascent Duration	Descent Duration	Total Time
Total Distance Covered		No. Of Steps

Companions

Weather

Enjoyment ○○○○○○○○○○
Views ○○○○○○○○○○
Difficulty ○○○○○○○○○○

Highlights

Notes

WHITTON HILL

Height (m): 74m
OS Grid Reference: NT 92810 34584
Flush Bracket Number: S7468

| Date | Parking ★★★★★ | Map Ref: /147\ |

Ascent Start Time | **Trig Time**

Descent Start Time | **Finish Time**

Ascent Duration | **Descent Duration** | **Total Time**

Total Distance Covered | **No. Of Steps**

Companions

Weather

Enjoyment ○○○○○○○○○○
Views ○○○○○○○○○○
Difficulty ○○○○○○○○○○

Highlights

Notes

WIND HILL

Height (m): 231m
OS Grid Reference: NY 68706 88830
Flush Bracket Number: S8031

Date	Parking	Map Ref: 148

Ascent Start Time		Trig Time	

Descent Start Time		Finish Time	

Ascent Duration	Descent Duration	Total Time

Total Distance Covered	No. Of Steps

Companions

Weather

Enjoyment ○ ○ ○ ○ ○ ○ ○ ○ ○ ○
Views ○ ○ ○ ○ ○ ○ ○ ○ ○ ○
Difficulty ○ ○ ○ ○ ○ ○ ○ ○ ○ ○

Highlights

Notes

WINDY GYLE

Height (m): 621m
OS Grid Reference: NT 85537 15214
Flush Bracket Number: S7999

Date	Parking ★ ★ ★ ★ ★	Map Ref: /149\

Ascent Start Time | **Trig Time**

Descent Start Time | **Finish Time**

Ascent Duration | **Descent Duration** | **Total Time**

Total Distance Covered | **No. Of Steps**

Companions

Weather

- Enjoyment ○ ○ ○ ○ ○ ○ ○ ○ ○ ○
- Views ○ ○ ○ ○ ○ ○ ○ ○ ○ ○
- Difficulty ○ ○ ○ ○ ○ ○ ○ ○ ○ ○

Highlights

Notes

WINNOWSHILL COMMON

Height (m): 314m
OS Grid Reference: NY 98172 54754
Flush Bracket Number: S6497

Date	Parking ★★★★★	Map Ref: /150\
Ascent Start Time		Trig Time
Descent Start Time		Finish Time
Ascent Duration	Descent Duration	Total Time
Total Distance Covered		No. Of Steps
Companions		

Weather

Enjoyment ○○○○○○○○○○
Views ○○○○○○○○○○
Difficulty ○○○○○○○○○○

Highlights

Notes

WINSHIELDS

Height (m): 345m
OS Grid Reference: NY 74213 67564
Flush Bracket Number: S6489

Date	Parking ★★★★★	Map Ref: /151\

Ascent Start Time | **Trig Time**

Descent Start Time | **Finish Time**

Ascent Duration | **Descent Duration** | **Total Time**

Total Distance Covered | **No. Of Steps**

Companions

Weather

Enjoyment ○○○○○○○○○○
Views ○○○○○○○○○○
Difficulty ○○○○○○○○○○

Highlights

Notes

WREIGHILL PIKE

Height (m): 219m
OS Grid Reference: NT 98084 02183
Flush Bracket Number: S8035

Date	Parking ★ ★ ★ ★ ★	Map Ref: /152\
Ascent Start Time		Trig Time
Descent Start Time		Finish Time
Ascent Duration	Descent Duration	Total Time
Total Distance Covered		No. Of Steps

Companions

Weather

Enjoyment ○ ○ ○ ○ ○ ○ ○ ○ ○ ○
Views ○ ○ ○ ○ ○ ○ ○ ○ ○ ○
Difficulty ○ ○ ○ ○ ○ ○ ○ ○ ○ ○

Highlights

Notes

Ready for your next adventure?

Keeping a log book is a fantastic way of recording your memories - and we have published a number of adventure log books available on Amazon. Simply scan the QR code to find out more!

Herbert Publishing is an independent husband & wife publisher on Amazon. We research & produce all of our books ourselves, retailing them through the Amazon platform.
If you like our books please consider leaving a review as this really helps our business.
We are constantly looking to expand our logbook series into new areas & niches, if you have any suggestions or ideas please send us an email!
info@herbertpublishing.com
Enjoy your hiking!

Printed in Great Britain
by Amazon